"Scott Hahn, one of our finest biblical theologians, has given us an important and timely reflection on a central mystery of our faith—how we die and rise in Jesus Christ and our hope in the resurrection of the body. This book reminds us that we are made for glory, for eternity in the beautiful city of God. I pray that it will lead many to seek to grow in holiness and love and to know that we are a people made for heaven."

MOST REVEREND JOSÉ H. GOMEZ
Archbishop of Los Angeles

"Hahn has written a book about a topic that affects every single person on this planet: death. It is clear from these pages that his great desire is for readers to understand the truth about themselves, about God, and about their supernatural destiny to be with him in heaven, soul and body. Dr. Hahn helps us see the logical and beautiful consequences of that reality. *Hope to Die* is erudite while readable, provocative but not polemical, compelling yet gentle."

FR. SEBASTIAN WHITE, O.P.
Editor in Chief, Magnificat

"Scott Hahn and Emily Stimpson Chapman provide a compelling and nourishing account of our reasons to hope in the promise of our own bodily resurrection. Written with intelligence and deep faith, *Hope to Die* is a testament to the enduring truth that, in Christ Jesus, we shall rise again."

FR. MATT MALONE, S.J.
Editor in Chief, America *Magazine*

"Our culture has lost the basic understanding of the human person made in the image and likeness of God. We see this so often when it comes to the life issues. But what about the dignity of the human person when it comes to death? We need a greater understanding and appreciation for what the Church teaches us in this area. And She has so much to offer, especially, as Dr. Hahn explains, in the gift that is St. John Paul II's Theology of the Body. This book is an important resource not only for those in ministry but for all Catholics who want to better understand and appreciate our dignity from conception until natural death and beyond."

TERESA TOMEO
Author and Radio Host of Catholic Connection *and*
The Catholic View for Women

"*Hope to Die* questions the meaning of 'resurrection of the body'—a belief that we all pledge when we recite the creed and hardly know what we are saying. This is a book that should be read *by* those who want to prepare for death and *to* those who are preparing others for death. You will learn what the age old (but fading) determination to bury the dead reveals about life and death—and you will likely re-think the practice of cremation. You will encounter the most pertinent passages in Scripture, you will taste the wisdom of saints, and you will ponder illuminating analogies. And greater understanding, hope, and consolation will be yours."

JANET SMITH
Author of Self-Gift: Humanae Vitae and the
Thought of John Paul II

"A wise Catholic theologian once said that death is the only thing we really have to look forward to. Scott Hahn beautifully explains the truth inside that paradox, and in doing so leads us into a deeper appreciation of both creation and redemption."

GEORGE WEIGEL

Distinguished Senior Fellow and William E. Simon Chair in Catholic Studies, Ethics and Public Policy Center

"What are we living for? What would we die for? What are we doing not only with our lives but with our bodies? Do we ask these questions? We must. *Hope to Die* helps us see all in its proper light—we are created by God, meant to return to him. Every inch of us belongs to him, the parts seen and unseen. This book will help us be the Christian people we are called to be."

KATHRYN JEAN LOPEZ

Senior Fellow, National Review Institute and Editor at Large, National Review; *Author of* A Year with the Mystics

"In *Hope to Die*, Scott Hahn extends this invitation to *die* with wonder, reverence, and *hope* for the body. From Genesis to Revelation, prophets to saints, theologians to mystics, Hahn weaves a persuasive case for reverence of your body that excludes both extremes of profanity and idolatry. *Hope to Die* is the patient, tender, but weighty explanation of *why* we honor the flesh that awaits its resurrection, redemption, and divinization."

DAMON OWENS

Founder of JoyTOB.org and Former Executive Director of the Theology of the Body Institute

HOPE TO DIE

HOPE TO DIE

THE CHRISTIAN MEANING OF DEATH
AND THE RESURRECTION OF THE BODY

☩

SCOTT HAHN

WITH EMILY STIMPSON CHAPMAN

EMMAUS ROAD
PUBLISHING

Steubenville, Ohio
www.EmmausRoad.org

Emmaus Road Publishing
1468 Parkview Circle
Steubenville, Ohio 43952

Library of Congress Control Number: 2020933583
ISBN 978-1-64585-030-4

Cover design and layout by Emily Demary
Cover image: *The Resurrection* (1715) by Sebastiano Ricci, Dulwich
Picture Gallery, Dulwich, South London

To Rob Corzine, friend and confidant

And to Fred and Molly Lou Hahn, Fred and Mayme Hahn,
R. Walker and Elmina Robb of beloved memory

Requiescat in Pace

Table of Contents

The Christian's Last Passover

The Christian meaning of death is revealed in the light of the *Paschal mystery* of the death and resurrection of Christ in whom resides our only hope. . . .

For the Christian the day of death inaugurates, *at the end of his sacramental life*, the fulfillment of his new birth begun at Baptism, the definitive "conformity" to "the image of the Son" conferred by the anointing of the Holy Spirit, and participation in the feast of the Kingdom which was anticipated in the Eucharist—even if final purifications are still necessary for him in order to be clothed with the nuptial garment.

The Church who, as Mother, has borne the Christian sacramentally in her womb during his earthly pilgrimage, accompanies him at his journey's end, in order to surrender him "into the Father's hands." She offers to the Father, in Christ, the child of his grace, and she commits to the earth, in hope, the seed of the body that will rise in glory.

Catechism of the Catholic Church 1681–1683

INTRODUCTION

A FITTING RESPONSE
TO THE BODY

In 1982, I preached my first sermon at a funeral. I was just recently ordained, and my grandmother had passed away, so my family wanted me to preside at the ceremony. Many of the details about the funeral are lost in the fog of time. But I remember one thing clearly.

During the sermon, I preached on Jesus's words in John 11:25: "I am the resurrection and the life." At some point, I mentioned that my grandmother's body—the very same body that had lived and worked and loved in life—would one day be resurrected. The body that was dead would live. The flesh that was already beginning to decay would be transfigured and enter into a life more real and more glorious than it had ever known on earth.

This is the ancient teaching of Christianity and one of the fundamental beliefs expressed in the Apostles' Creed: "I believe in . . . the resurrection of the body, and life everlasting." Protestants and Catholics alike profess that Creed, and so when I mentioned it, I didn't think I was saying anything all that shocking.

After the funeral was over, though, my mother came up to me—my faithful, practicing Christian mother—and said, "You don't really believe that, do you?"

"Believe what?" I asked.

"That these bodies will be resurrected," she replied.

In the moment, her skepticism surprised me. But, over the years, the more I've realized she's not alone. Most of us don't really believe in the resurrection of the body. Or we struggle to believe it. Quoting Saint Augustine, the Catechism acknowledges this struggle, stating:

> From the beginning, Christian faith in the resurrection has met with incomprehension and opposition. 'On no point does the Christian faith encounter more opposition than on the resurrection of the body.' It is very commonly accepted that the life of the human person continues in a spiritual fashion after death. But how can we believe that this body, so clearly mortal, could rise to everlasting life? (CCC 996)

I think many of us believe we'll get a new body once we enter into eternal life or on Judgment Day. But we don't see how this body—this weak, mortal body that eats and sleeps, catches cold and bleeds—could possibly be resurrected to eternal life. Surely God has better material he can work with?

Again, the Creed says otherwise. And in the original Greek, it says it even more explicitly. The first Christians who composed the Creed didn't use the Greek word for body: *soma*. They used the Greek word for flesh: *sarx*. Every time we pray the Creed, that's what we say: I believe in the resurrection of the flesh—of this flesh, of my flesh, of my tired, aging, imperfect flesh. I believe that this body will one day stand before the throne of Christ and worship him with all the angels and saints. Yet, for all that we say it, so few of us really live it.

In life, we don't treat our bodies like sacred temples that belong in the heavenly courts. We either abuse them—eating too much or too little, denying them sleep, denying them rest, filling them with toxic substances, and giving them over to immoral purposes. Or, we worship them—doing everything we can to recreate them into some cultural ideal. Sometimes, we do both, while also doing all we can to keep the signs of bodily weakness and aging at bay. Death, almost everyone agrees, is the one great evil.

But when death inevitably comes, how do we treat those bodies?

Today, more and more of us burn them. We don't bury our bodies. We don't treat them as our ancestors did, with reverence and care. Instead, we destroy the flesh in fire, crush the bones that withstand the flames, and then often scatter the remains, destroying all evidence that this body—this holy body in which God's Spirit dwelt—ever existed.

We live like materialists. We die like Nihilists. And this is a problem.

A Singular Witness

Before I go any further, I want to make a couple things clear. First, this book is not meant to be yet another contribution to the culture wars. I have great respect for those making the case in the public square for the dignity of the human body, the sanctity of human life, and the truth of our sexuality. This book takes those points as a given. But I'm not writing this book to engage in those debates.

Second, if you're reading this book and have a loved one who was cremated, please don't think I'm here to condemn them for their decision or make you question their salvation. I'm not. People aren't lost to God when they're lost at sea, and they're not lost to God when they're cremated. The Church now permits cremation, and I'm not here to tell the Church she's wrong. At the same time, the increasingly widespread practice of cremation seems to me to be a symptom of a very real problem in how we see our bodies, in life and in death. And that way of seeing has consequences.

The central truth of the Christian faith is that Jesus Christ, God-made-man, rose again. As the French author, poet, and mystic Madeleine Delbrêl so beautifully put it, Jesus's first disciples left Jerusalem:

> Not to proclaim in the first place and loudest the universal love that Jesus taught them, the justice for the little ones [and] for the weak and the oppressed . . . but to proclaim first and loudest that Jesus Christ, the man who was our friend . . . who was spat upon, mocked, struck, and scourged, who was tortured amidst laughter and hung upon a cross, who was bled

dry, who let out his last breath with a moan, who froze upon the cross [and] who no one doubted was dead . . . this Jesus Christ is risen.[1]

That's what sets Christianity apart from so many other faiths. Hinduism proclaims compassion. Buddhism urges people to perform works of charity. Islam calls people to worship the one true God.

But only Christianity says the one we follow *is* God. He became a man, walked among us, suffered and died on a cross, and then rose again from the dead, *in that same body* . . . a body that bore the marks of the nails and the spear.

But there's more. Christianity also says that everyone who believes in that resurrected man will walk the same path. We will suffer. We will die. And we will rise again. What happened to his body will happen to our bodies. Where he went, we will follow—in spirit and in flesh.

That belief changes everything. It *changed* everything. The Catholic author Patricia Snow writes:

From the primary gospel of the Resurrection . . . the secondary gospel flowed: morality of every kind that touches on the human person. Everything that Jesus taught that Western modernity approves—consideration for the neighbor and the child, the marginal and the oppressed—and everything he taught that modernity resists—the importance of sexual purity, for example, as something inseparable from spiritual

---

[1] Madeleine Delbrêl, *We, the Ordinary People of the Streets* (Grand Rapids, MI: Eerdmans, 2000), 186–87.

health—follows, eventually if not immediately, from the revelation of the resurrection . . . If the whole man is immortal, a comprehensive morality follows. If religion is simply spiritual—if the body is a temporary expedient and only the soul perdures—ultimately, everything may be permitted.[2]

From the doctrine of the Resurrection flowed a morality. And from a morality flowed a culture. Michelangelo and Fra Angelico, Bach and Mozart, Shakespeare and Mendel—art, music, literature, science, all of it that we call great was rooted in the idea that man was destined for more, in body and soul, and that such a destiny made the world—his home—sacred. It made matter sacred. It made life sacred.

Today, though, in the post-Christian West, truths that once seemed self-evident are quickly being forgotten. We've forgotten for what these bodies of ours were made. We've forgotten for whom they were made. And that forgetting shows in how we live, how we die, and how we treat those who've died.

A Fitting Response

The New Evangelization—the Church's mission to re-evangelize the de-Christianized—is a campaign that must take place on many fronts. Its success requires a sustained catechesis touching on every aspect of human life: from how

---

[2] Patricia Snow, "The Body and Christian Burial: The Question of Cremation," *Communio* 39 (Fall 2012): 398–412.

we worship and pray to how we love, eat, work, and, *not unimportantly*, how we bury our dead.

How we treat our bodies in death matters. Not because God can't work around whatever we do to our bodies. He can. But rather because how Christians deal with death—how we think about death, talk about death, and treat the dead—is a form of witness. It is a witness to a materialist, nihilist, radically confused world about the holiness of our bodies and the life for which we are meant. We were not made for death. We were made for life.

The purpose of this book is to help you see that. It's to help you see more deeply into the logic that underlies the Church's teachings on death and the body—the logic of love—so that you can understand why she has always, even now, urged Catholics to bury, not burn, the dead. Burial is not strictly necessary. The Church has been clear on that. But it is fitting. The Church also has been clear on that. In this book, we'll explore why it's fitting to bury the dead, and why this understanding of "fittingness" has implications that go well beyond what we do to our bodies after life has left them.

We'll also give you the tools you need to share this understanding of death and the body with the ones you love.

So often, the most important conversations about faith happen at one of three moments in life: at births, at weddings, and at deaths. Birth opens up the heart, helping us realize that our bodies are so much more than we thought, and sexuality is so much more powerful than we realized. Weddings do something similar, showing us that love is so much more powerful, beautiful, and demanding than we imagined. And death? Death teaches us that we're weaker than we thought—we're mortal—and there must be something more than this. There must be a love that is stronger than death. That type of love is the deepest longing of all our hearts. It's the love for which we were made. And as life draws to a close, our hearts long for it more, not less.

When those moments come for the people you love, my hope is that this book helps you enter more deeply and fruitfully into the conversations that surround that moment.

First things first, though. In order to understand that we were made for life, not death, we first have to know what life and death are.

CHAPTER 1

✝

LIFE AND DEATH

When my daughter Hannah was in high school, she was fascinated with zombies. I didn't get it. And honestly (sorry, Hannah), I thought it was a little weird. Then, I started realizing she wasn't alone. There was the hit TV show *The Walking Dead*, the best-selling novel *World War Z*, and even a movie called *Pride and Prejudice and Zombies* (which, no, I haven't seen and can't even begin to imagine).

Over the past fifteen years or so, our culture has become obsessed with the concept of the dead who live. And while at first that obsession might seem "weird," there's actually something to it—something beyond blood and gore. At the heart of all those zombie stories, from *The Zombie Survival Guide* to *Shaun of the Dead*, their creators are asking the same two questions: What does it mean to live? And what does it mean to die?

I don't think it's a coincidence that the low-budget cult movie that launched the zombie phenomena, *Night of the Living Dead* (filmed near my hometown of Pittsburgh), was made in 1968—a time when all the old answers Christianity gave about life and death were suddenly suspect.

But over the past five decades, the world hasn't just questioned the answers Christianity gives; it's forgotten them. An understanding of how the Church sees living and dying has been lost by much of the world, even those parts of the world that were once deeply Christian. We don't know who we are anymore, and that cultural forgetting is one of the driving needs behind the New Evangelization.

Let's start addressing that need here by going back to the beginning, to Genesis, to the first page in humanity's story of life and death.

The Breath of Life

Every Sunday, in Mass, we recite the Nicene Creed. There are three sections to the Creed: one devoted to the Father, one devoted to the Son, and one devoted to the Holy Spirit. At the beginning of the third section, we address the Holy Spirit as "the Lord, the giver of life." The "Lord" part is straightforward enough. The Holy Spirit is Lord because he is God, one of the Three Divine Persons that make up the Holy Trinity. But what does it mean that he is the "giver of life?"

The Book of Genesis answers that question in two ways.

First, in Genesis 1:1–2, we read: "In the beginning God created the heavens and the earth. The earth was without form and void, and darkness was upon the face of the deep; and the Spirit of God was moving over the face of the waters."

This passage tells us that the Holy Spirit is the giver of physical life, of what the Greeks called *bios*. Trees grow, flowers bloom, and our hearts beat all by the power of the Holy Spirit. All that lives, moves, and has being—to paraphrase Acts 17:28—does so because of the Spirit. He gives *bios*, natural biological life.

But, there's life . . . and then there's life. That is, there's *bios* and then there's *zoe*. *Zoe* is the word the Greek translators of the Old Testament used in Genesis 2:7: "Then the LORD God formed man of dust from the ground, and breathed into his nostrils the breath of life [*zoe*]; and man became a living being."

Unlike *bios*, *zoe* conveys so much more than mere physical existence. God didn't just breathe air into Adam's nostrils; he breathed *life*—spiritual life, eternal life, divine life. He breathed his own life into Adam. He gave Adam the life that from all eternity the Father is always communicatirg to the Son and that the Son is receiving and communicating right back to the Father.[1] That life is so whole, so complete, it's actually a Person: the Third Person of the Trinity. God breathed his Spirit into Adam, and that made it possible for him to live a life that wasn't just natural, but supernatural.

Filled with *zoe*, Adam knew God intimately, familiarly, as a son knows his father, from the first moment of existence. He also imaged God, much as a son images his father, although his resemblance wasn't physical; it was spiritual and intellectual.

---

[1] See CCC 375: "The Church, interpreting the symbolism of biblical language in an authentic way, in the light of the New Testament and Tradition, teaches that our first parents, Adam and Eve, were constituted in an original 'state of holiness and justice' [Cf. Council of Trent (1546): DS 1511]. This grace of original holiness was 'to share in . . . divine life' [Cf. LG 2]."

God made Adam in his image, which meant Adam had the ability to reason, to create, to know right from wrong, and to give his life in love to and for another. He also had oneness—what St. Augustine called *memoria* or "memory." Even though God is Three, he also is One; in a similar way, although as the years passed Adam might look different, think differently, and feel different, he would still be the same Adam. There would be an inner unity to who he was yesterday and who he would be tomorrow. Memory would hold past, present, and future together in one person.

Filled with God's life and made in God's image, Adam was capable of truly living, both naturally and supernaturally. That is, it was possible for him to not just copulate with Eve but to *know* Eve, to choose her and love her and care for her as his bride.

It was also possible for Adam to not just sire children but to *father* children—to be a father to Cain and Abel and Seth in a way similar to how God was a father to him.

Most importantly, it was possible for Adam to worship God in Spirit and truth in this life and the next—to participate in the very life of God for all eternity, remembering forever and always the blessings of God and the care God extended to him every day of his life.

God gave Adam existence, but he also gave Adam *life*. He gave Adam the ability to live a fully human life, with love, friendship, family, and community. And he gave Adam the ability to live a life that was more than human, that was divine, with the Spirit of God dwelling in his soul.

But then Adam went and lost that gift of divine life, for himself and for all his descendants.

The First Death

When we understand the distinction between *bios* and *zoe*, God's words to Adam and Eve in Genesis 2:16–17 start to make a lot more sense. There, God lays out the ground rules for life in Eden, explaining, "You may freely eat of every tree in the garden; but of the tree of the knowledge of good and evil you shall not eat, for in the day that you eat of it you shall die."

In the original Hebrew, even more emphasis is placed on the word "die." The literal translation of that passage is "die the death."

God sounds serious there. Deadly serious. Yet in the very next chapter, without missing a beat, Adam and Eve eat the fruit God warned them not to eat . . . and nothing happens. At least seemingly. They don't gag and choke. They don't fall into a faint. They don't drop dead on the spot.

But when you realize there are two kinds of life—*bios* and *zoe*—you also realize there are two kinds of death—bodily death and spiritual death. Adam and Eve didn't die physically that day in the Garden, but they did die spiritually. They lost something far more precious than natural life: they lost supernatural life, divine life, the gift of sanctifying grace in their soul.

Had Adam not listened to his wife, had he protested, called the serpent on his lies, and fought back, he might have been physically attacked by the serpent and lost his physical life. But he would have held on to the more important gift. He still would have possessed sanctifying grace, the gift of divine sonship. He would have had *zoe*.

Adam didn't fight back, though, and that failure brought death into the world. First, it brought spiritual death, depriving not only himself and his bride of sanctifying grace, but also all their descendants—the entire human race. That's what original sin is. It's not a thing we do; it's a thing we lack. It's human nature deprived of divine life. And every human ever born has inherited that deprived nature from our first parents. We're born physically alive, but spiritually dead.

From the first death, the second death followed. After bringing spiritual death into the world, Adam's sin brought physical death, as well. Not immediately. But eventually. Paul tells us this in Romans 5:12, writing, "Therefore as sin came into the world through one man and death through sin, and so death spread to all men because all men sinned."

That seems backwards, like sin should have spread with death, not death with sin. But if original sin is the loss of divine life, if men are born deprived, not depraved, then we're born lacking the life we were meant to have. We are born dead, divinely speaking. So spiritual death spreads to all Adam's progeny, who receive natural life at birth, but not divine life. And as the spiritually dead commit sins of their own, physical death spreads.

From our deprived human nature, a deprived life follows—a life that is not all it was meant to be, naturally or supernaturally, physically or spiritually. The physical death humanity experiences as a consequence of sin becomes like an anti-sacrament, a visible sign of the invisible state of the deprived, spiritually dead soul.

The Walking Dead

Unfortunately, a deprived human nature isn't the only thing we inherited from Adam and Eve. We also inherited concupiscence, which is a tendency to sin. Adam's fall from grace left all his descendants with a darkened intellect, a weakened will, and disordered affections and appetites.

This means it's harder for us than it was for Adam and Eve before the Fall to know the good, choose the good, do the good, and even want the good. Baptism (which we'll talk more about in the next chapter) restores God's life to our souls, but it doesn't take away the tendency to sin. It doesn't restore to us the clarity of mind, the strength of will, and the rightness of desire that Adam and Eve had in the beginning. This means that, at some point or another, we all commit sins of our own. We choose our will over God's.

That choice can dim the life of God in our soul so that we become even more susceptible to even greater sin. Or, when the choices are bad enough—when they involve grave matter, full knowledge, and free consent—they can kill God's life in us entirely. This is what mortal sin is. It is spiritual death.

Recently, I was watching the old M. Night Shyamalan movie *The Sixth Sense* and was struck by what the young character Cole revealed to his psychiatrist, Malcolm—not just that he sees dead people, but more significantly, that they don't know they're dead. They see what they want to see. They hear what they want to hear. They ignore the reality of their own death, even though it is staring them in the face.

This is the world in which we live. Only, the people who don't realize they're dead aren't physically dead; they're spiritually dead. Some are unbaptized. Others are baptized but have fallen into mortal sin. But the spiritually dead are everywhere—on our streets and in our schools, in our workplaces and even in our parishes.

All around us are people not living the life they were made to live, who don't have the life of God dwelling in their souls. They are the living dead—the reality to which all those zombie movies point. And they don't even know it. They see what they want to see. They hear what they want to hear.

Importantly, these people aren't less dead than those who are physically dead but alive in Christ. They are *more* dead. They are *more* dead than the saints, *more* dead than the souls in purgatory. This is the type of death we should fear. Jesus warned: "And do not fear those who kill the body but cannot kill the soul; rather fear him who can destroy both soul and body in hell" (Matt 10:28).

Yet, as the sixth-century bishop, St. Julian of Toledo, noted, that's not a warning most of us heed:

> Everyone fears death of the flesh, few fear death of the soul. All are preoccupied with the coming of death of the flesh, which sooner or later, certainly must come. And for this they weary themselves. Destined to die, humankind struggles to avoid dying, and yet, destined to live forever, they do not labor to avoid sinning. And when they struggle to avoid death, they labor in vain; in fact, the most they obtain is that death is deferred, not avoided; if rather they refrain from sinning, their toil will cease and they will live forever. Oh that we could incite humankind, ourselves included, to be lovers of everlasting life as

much as they are lovers of the life that passes away![2]

So, we strive to avoid the death that is unavoidable, but we don't strive to avoid the death that is avoidable. We fail to see, as St. Paul did, "to live is Christ, and to die is gain" (Phil 1:21). For a soul filled with divine life, the death of the body is the beginning of our real life, the life for which we were always made. The death of the soul in sin—sin for which it never repents—is the end of everything for which we've always longed.

The creators of shows like *The Walking Dead* and *Night of the Living Dead* get a great deal wrong about life and death, but they also get a great deal right. A person can be alive, but not alive. A person can be dead, but not dead. There is more to life than simply moving and talking and consuming. And there is more to death than the cessation of breathing.

Each of us faces a choice every moment of every day. When we choose God—his laws, his wills, and his way—we choose life. And when we choose ourselves—our laws, our wills, our way—we choose death.

We don't make those choices as disembodied spirits, though. We make them in and through our bodies, bodies that can hold both death and life within them.

---

[2] Julian of Toledo, *Foreknowledge of the World to Come,* trans. Tommaso Stancati, O.P. (New York: Newman Press, 2010), 383–84.

CHAPTER 2

THE BODY: THE SACRAMENT OF THE PERSON

One of the greatest blessings of my life was sitting by my father's side as he breathed his last. I arrived at the hospital early in the morning and found that my mom had been there, sitting up with him, all night. She left the room to get breakfast, and I took her place by his side. She wasn't gone long, but in the twenty minutes it took for her to get some food, my father's breathing grew more labored, slowed, and finally stopped.

But saying it "stopped" isn't right. That would be like saying a symphony "stopped." Symphonies don't just stop. They end on a clear and resounding note. There is no doubt when the symphony is over. That's how it was with my dad. When he took his last breath and then exhaled one final time, it wasn't any ordinary breath. It was clearly his last. The life almost audibly went out of him. His soul had left his body.

19

At that moment, I dropped to my knees in prayer and grief. I'd lost my dad, and I wanted the whole world to stop turning. I then closed his eyes and waited for my mom to return. Those moments were heartbreaking, but they also were blessed. It wasn't disturbing to be there with my dad; it was beautiful. Sitting there, I knew as wholly and completely as I knew my own name, that I was in the presence of something sacred: a body that had given life to my own body, a body that had been restored to life through Baptism, a body that would one day rise again.

The Sacrament of the Person

This is the way the Church calls us to see all bodies—living and dead. If we're not careful, though, it's easy to fall into the trap that human beings have been falling into for thousands of years, thinking of bodies as nothing more than matter, disposable, unimportant, separate from our real and true selves and disconnected from our soul.

This is how Diogenes—the more-than-half-mad ancient Greek philosopher—saw his body back in the third century before Christ. He told his followers that after he died, he wanted his body thrown over the city walls so that the wild beasts outside could devour it. He would be dead, he reasoned, so what use would he have for his body at that point? This is also the understanding of the body that underlies a popular saying (wrongly attributed to C. S. Lewis), which asserts, "You don't have a soul. You are a soul. You have a body."

Wrong. You are a soul, yes. But you also are a body. You are both because you are a human person, and a human person, the Church teaches, is a union of body and soul. The soul animates the body, and the body, as Pope St. John Paul II so beautifully put it, "expresses the person." The body is the sign of the person or, even more accurately, the sacrament of the person. It "reveals the living soul," making the invisible visible and enabling you to communicate to the world who you are: what you think, feel, know, fear, desire, and love.[1]

Again, though, this isn't how our world sees the body. When most people today think of the body, they think of it like Diogenes or the fake C. S. Lewis. They don't see a divine purpose to it. They don't see it as a sacrament. It's not part of who we are; it's just something we have. And so, like any possession, the world tells us we can treat it however we want to treat it. We can worship it or we can abuse it. We can care for it or we can neglect it. We can change it cosmetically or move heaven and earth trying to prevent it from change. What we do with it, whom we give it to, whether we attempt to prolong its existence or cut it short, and finally, whether we burn it or bury it—all that is up to us. When the body—the flesh—is devoid of divine meaning, anything goes.

Again, though, the Church knows better. The Church knows the body has the potential to be more than useful, more than good, more than beautiful. It knows the body has the potential to be holy.

This holiness, in one way, is natural to all men and women because our bodies, like everything else in creation,

---

[1] John Paul II, *Man and Woman He Created Them: A Theology of the Body,* trans. Michael Waldstein (Boston: Paulist Press, 2006), 183.

proclaim some truth about our Creator. The twelfth-century Doctor of the Church, St. Hildegard of Bingen, expressed this beautifully in her final book of visions, *The Book of Divine Works*, noting that, "just as a coin reveals the ruler who minted it," God "set his signature on all his work in the human form."[2]

She then meditates on some of the ways the body does this, writing:

> For in the circle of the brain, God reveals his lordship, for the brain governs and rules the whole body. In the hair of the head, God designates his potential, which is his beauty, just as the hair beautifies the head. In the eyebrows, he demonstrates his might, for the brows protect a person's eyes, keep harmful things out of them, and set off the beauty of the face . . . In the eyes, God declares his knowledge, but which he foresees and foreknows all. . . . And, in the hearing, God discloses all the sounds of praise of the secret mysteries and angelic hosts, among who God himself is praised.[3]

All this is to say that in their strength, intelligence, power, and beauty, our bodies point to God's strength, power, intelligence, and beauty. In their goodness, they testify to God's goodness. In their capacity to create and build and grow things, they echo a God who is the Creator of all. And,

---

[2] Barbara Newman, "Commentary on the Johannine Prologue: Hildegard of Bingen," *Theology Today* 60, no. 1 (Apr 2003): 23, 29.

[3] Newman, "Commentary on the Johannine Prologue," 23.

in their ability to bring forth new life, they image a God who is life-giving love. Through it all, as a witness to the Holy Trinity, our bodies have a natural holiness.

The Consequences of Sin

In the beginning of humanity's history, this natural holiness wasn't hard to perceive. In the Garden, before the Fall, Adam and Eve, in both body and soul, imaged God as he made them to image him. In his classic treatise, *On the Incarnation*, St. Athanasius says this is how God revealed himself to man, so that "through this gift of God's likeness in themselves they may be able to perceive the Image absolute, that is the Word himself, and through Him, to apprehend the Father."[4]

God also gave Adam and Eve three gifts, which helped perfect his image in them. The first was the gift of immortality, which means their bodies possessed the ability to live forever, to never die. The second was the gift of integrity—that is, their bodies were perfectly subject to their reason, never their passions. And the third gift was infused knowledge, meaning that without being taught, Adam and Eve knew truths about themselves and God that many of us never know in this life, not even with the help of Divine Revelation and years of theological study. Adam and Eve understood the deepest truths about themselves and God like the rest of us breathe.

---

[4] Athanasius, *On the Incarnation*, trans. and edited by a religious of C.S.M.V., 2nd ed. (Crestwood, NY: St. Vladimir's Seminary Press, 1993), 38.

Because of these gifts, Adam and Eve could look at each other and see God. They also could look at the works of creation that surrounded them and see God. They weren't God. Creation wasn't God. But who God was and what he wanted of them was, in a sense, incarnate in the world around them. It was staring them in the face all the time.

Unfortunately for us, as we discussed in Chapter 1, they closed their eyes. They chose to ignore what they saw and stepped out of God's will. They then experienced the consequences of that choice as a whole person, body and soul. First they lost divine life in their souls and said goodbye to the gifts of integrity and infused knowledge. Then, eventually, they lost physical life in their bodies, for their spiritual death also cost them the gift of immortality. With their reason now unable to govern their passions and their understanding clouded by sin, Adam, Eve, and their descendants could no longer clearly perceive God's image in themselves or be the image of God they were made to be.

This doesn't mean man, in body and soul, wasn't still made in the image of God. Sin can't change the fact that God made us in his image. But it does mean we weren't acting like that image. The mirror had become clouded by sin, and when we looked in it, a very poor image of God looked back at us.

To make matters worse, we couldn't clean the mirror. We tried. God gave us laws to follow that were meant to help us—both the natural law written in men's hearts and the law of the Old Covenant, written in stone for the Israelites. But both were laws that, in our fallen state, apart from grace, we couldn't keep.

The more humanity sinned, the more the image of God

was marred in them, until finally, to do for us what we couldn't do, God sent us the redeemer promised in Genesis 3:15, the one who would crush the head of the serpent and destroy death's power over us. That redeemer was Jesus Christ.

St. Athanasius explains:

> What else could he possibly do, being God, but renew his image in mankind? And how could this be done save by the coming of the very Image himself, our Savior Jesus Christ? Men could not have done it, for they are only made after the Image; nor could angels have done it, for they are not the images of God. The Word of God came in his own Person, because it was He alone, the Image of the Father, who could recreate man made after the Image.[5]

The Effects of the Incarnation

Before we go any further, it's important to remember that God's promise in Genesis 3:15, wasn't Plan B for creation. The forbidden fruit sampling going on in the Garden didn't catch God by surprise during the second week of creation. And after our first parents' immortal bodies became mortal, God the Father didn't have to scramble to come up with a new plan for redeeming humanity or call in any favors from God the Son.

God is eternal. He is outside of time. He always knew

---

[5] Athanasius, *On the Incarnation*, 39–41.

how events would unfold in Eden, which means the plan for our salvation that had the Second Person of the Trinity entering the world to renew the image of God in man was always Plan A.

By doing that, by becoming man, assuming human flesh and a human nature, St. Athanasius tells us, Jesus, the Son of God, "sanctified the body."[6] Just like Jesus's descending into the waters and allowing John to baptize him made the water holy, the Son of God descending into a human body and becoming man made the body holy. It imparted a new and greater dignity to human flesh. After the Incarnation, not only had the body been created by God; it had been assumed by God. It had been united to God. That union gave new value to every other human body.

It also gave us a new understanding of the human body, and why the human person is a union of body and soul, matter and spirit.

Before the Incarnation, man's singularity in the world— his existence as the only creature in creation to possess both a mortal body and an immortal rational soul—was a puzzle. He was flesh like the animals, but spirit like the angels. Visible and invisible came together in him. But why?

Jesus's coming answered that question. He not only reminds us that we were made in the image and likeness of God, but he shows us *the* image, himself, the prototype for who we were made to be. In him, we see who man really is. We also come to see that while we were made to be like him, we also were made for him to be like us. The plan was always for the uncreated to enter into the created so that

---

[6] Athanasius, *On the Incarnation*, 47.

the created could enter into the uncreated. We were always made to be the nexus, the point, connecting heaven and earth, temporal and eternal, creation and Creator.

Most importantly, the Incarnation set the stage for giving a holiness that is more than natural, that is actually supernatural, to every human body that unites itself to Christ.

From the moment Jesus began his public ministry, he made it clear that he had come to give back to man what had been lost in the Garden: *zoe.*

Referencing *zoe* a total of forty-three times in his Gospel, John tells us repeatedly that *zoe* is the life Jesus possesses, the life that Jesus is. "For as the Father has *zoe* in himself, so he has granted the Son also to have *zoe* in himself" (John 5:26). "I am the bread of *zoe*," Jesus says in John 6:48. Then, "I am the Resurrection and the *zoe*" (John 11:25), and "I am the way, the truth, and the *zoe*" (John 14:6).

Zoe is also what Jesus wants us to have. "I came that they might have *zoe* and have it abundantly," he says in John 10:10. And, "God so loved the world that he gave his only Son, that whoever believes in him should not perish but have eternal *zoe*," Jesus explains to Nicodemus in John 3:16.

Zoe, in many ways, is the ultimate gift of the Incarnation. It is the ultimate reason for the Incarnation. It's the why behind Jesus coming. But, unlike the new dignity all bodies take on through the Incarnation, *zoe* isn't imparted to all people automatically. It's imparted through Baptism.

In Baptism, we are born anew, receiving what Adam lost—the gift of divine life—into our souls once more. It's easy to dismiss Baptism as a mere symbol, but when you understand the difference between *bios* and *zoe* and between physical death and spiritual death, it becomes clear that the

Sacrament of Baptism is more than figurative or symbolic. There is an ontological reality to our resurrection.

In the waters of Baptism, we die and rise by being united to Christ's resurrected body. The divine life is restored to us so that the newly baptized person is more resurrected than Lazarus was. Lazarus got his natural, physical life back after four days. But in Baptism, we get our supernatural and divine life back, the life that Adam lost in the very beginning of time.

Baptism makes it possible for us to live the life for which God made us—a life that is more than natural—that is, in fact, supernatural. It also makes it possible for us to live a more fully human life, to enter more deeply into those things that make this earthly life worth living and have richer, more intimate connections with family and friends.

But Baptism doesn't just affect our souls; it affects our bodies, too.

Temples of the Holy Spirit

In all the sacraments, sanctifying grace—God's own life—comes to us through our bodies. In Baptism, in Confirmation, in Marriage, in Holy Orders, and above all, in the Eucharist, God's life enters into these bodies of ours through matter—water, wine, oil, a bishop's hands, a spouse's body—restoring the divine life that was lost by Adam and strengthening it within us. That grace divinizes our bodies. It makes them holy. It makes them temples. "Do you not know that you are God's temple and that God's Spirit dwells in you?" asks Paul in 1 Corinthians 3:16.

In every single baptized person who is not in a state of mortal sin, God lives. He dwells within us. All human life is sacred because it is a gift from God and because man is made in the image of God. But the bodies of the baptized have a holiness that comes from the sanctifying grace abiding within them. As C. S. Lewis once remarked in his famous lecture, "The Weight of Glory":

> Next to the Blessed Sacrament itself, your neighbor is the holiest object presented to your senses. If he is your Christian neighbor, he is holy in almost the same way [as the Blessed Sacrament], for in him also Christ *vere latitat*—the glorifier and the glorified, Glory Himself, is truly hidden.[7]

The closer and more intimate a person's union with Christ is, the more that holiness manifests in their body. Sometimes, in the bodies of saints such as St. Francis, St. Catherine of Siena, St. Pio of Pietrelcina, St. Joseph Cupertino, and many more, holiness manifests through signs and wonders like the stigmata, bilocation, and levitation. More often, it manifests through a person's ability to radiate the love of Christ. People who met St. Teresa of Calcutta often remarked that she was the most beautiful woman they'd ever met—not because she looked like a cover model (she didn't), but because the love of Christ shone forth from her weathered, wrinkled face.

Importantly, the holiness of the baptized body doesn't

---

[7] C. S. Lewis, "The Weight of Glory," *The Weight of Glory and Other Addresses* (New York: Macmillan, 1980), 19.

end with death. Grace continues to linger in the bodies and bones of those united to Christ. That's why Catholic cemeteries are considered holy ground. The bodies of the baptized are buried there. And those bodies are the seed of the resurrected body.

> What you sow does not come to life unless it dies. And what you sow is not the body which is to be, but a bare kernel, perhaps of wheat or of some other grain. But God gives it a body as he has chosen, and to each kind of seed its own body. (1 Cor 15: 26–38, 42–44)

In Genesis, as we saw, there is life and there is *life*; there is *bios* and *zoe*. There is also death and there is *death*; there is spiritual death and there is physical death. And, there are bodies and *bodies*. There are our present bodies, and there are our resurrected bodies.

Jesus promises to raise our bodies: "No one can come to me unless the Father who sent me draws him; and I will raise him up at the last day," he says in John 6:44. But he also promises to transform them, to glorify them, to deify them. "As was the man of dust, so are those who are of the dust," writes St. Paul, "and as is the man of heaven, so are those who are of heaven. Just as we have borne the image of the man of dust, we shall also bear the image of the man of heaven" (1 Cor 15:48–49).

This promise of resurrection is our hope. It is that on which we stake our life. It is what enables us, as Christians, to face death with courage and joy.

Before we explore just what that promise entails and

how God fulfills it, however, we need to look at how the resurrection was understood by those who first hoped in it—Abraham, Isaac, and Jacob—and how that hope shaped the way the ancient Israelites treated their dead.

CHAPTER 3

WAITING FOR A
BETTER COUNTRY

Endings are important. As an author, this is something I know. You work hard to make sure you end books on just the right note—that you leave your reader with some moment of resolution, illumination, or clarity.

Several years ago, I noticed something about the Book of Genesis: the ending felt—for lack of a better word—anticlimactic.

In Genesis 49, after being reunited with his beloved son Joseph, Jacob bestowed his blessing on his twelve sons, instructed them about what to do with his body, then "breathed his last, and was gathered to his people" (Gen 49:33). If I were the author of Genesis, that's where I would have wrapped things up. That last sentence neatly ties together the stories of all the Patriarchs told up to that point.

The book doesn't end there, though. Instead, in Genesis 50, it goes on to recount how Joseph and his brothers took their father's body back to the land of Canaan and buried it in the tomb where Abraham and Sarah, Isaac and Rebekah, and Jacob's first wife Leah were all buried. That chapter finally concludes with Joseph's death and the oath he made the Israelites swear:

> And Joseph said to his brothers, "I am about to die; but God will visit you, and bring you up out of this land to the land which he swore to Abraham, to Isaac, and to Jacob." Then Joseph took an oath of the sons of Israel, saying, "God will visit you, and you shall carry up my bones from here." So Joseph died, being a hundred and ten years old; and they embalmed him, and he was put in a coffin in Egypt. (Gen 50:24–26)

"And they embalmed him, and he was put in a coffin in Egypt." Okay. Writing up the burial details are not how I would have ended Genesis. It's not really how any author I know would have ended Genesis. Which is why, the more I thought about it, the more it seemed like either A) Somewhere along the way, ancient Israel lost the actual end of Genesis; or B) This is the end, and it's saying something incredibly important that my twenty-first-century ears can't seem to hear.

If I had to lay odds on which one it is—A or B—I'd go with B, because this isn't the only book of the Bible to end that way. Deuteronomy does something similar, ending with the death of Moses and his burial by God in the land of Moab. The Book of Joshua then does it again, concluding with Joshua's burial among his people in the hill country of Ephraim and, at long last, the burial of Joseph's bones at Shechem. So, of the first six books of the Bible, three of them (including the first and last books of the Pentateuch) end by telling us what they did with the Patriarchs' bodies.

To us, this doesn't seem like an important detail. To the ancient Israelites, it did. Why?

Nobody knows for sure. There's no clear answer to this puzzle. But I have a guess. It seems, in a sense, like they're waiting for something. That the end isn't the end. That Abraham, Isaac, and Jacob; Joseph, Moses, and Joshua are waiting for the real end to the story. And that end is the resurrection—their resurrection and the resurrection of all the dead.

Communion with the Dead

Just what exactly the ancient Israelites believed about death and the resurrection is not a settled question. On the one hand, there's no explicit teaching about the resurrection of the dead in the Books of the Law. There's no promise explicitly made in the Pentateuch about the life to come. A modern biblical scholar, simply reading the text of the Bible's first books and taking it at face value, could say that the ancient Israelites didn't believe in the resurrection of the dead. And in Jesus's time, that's what the Sadducees did say. So, on the surface, there's that.

On the other hand, if the ancient Israelites didn't believe in the resurrection of the dead, if they didn't believe in an afterlife, then they were pretty much the only people in the ancient world who thought that way. A belief in the life to come in the ancient world wasn't just widespread; it was universal. Everyone, from the Canaanites and Amorites to the Egyptians, Babylonians, and Assyrians, believed in some kind of life after death. There was more than an awareness of a life still to come; there was a fixation on what was to come.

Moreover, if the Israelites didn't believe in some kind of resurrection, their words and actions make no sense, because their behavior suggests they very much did believe in it.

When you look at the burial practices of ancient Israel, you see this. In his landmark two-volume survey *Israel: Its Life and Culture*, the theologian Johannes Pedersen details how ancient Israel, like its neighbors, kept its dead close. For centuries, the dead weren't buried far from community life; they were buried in the midst of community life—near or even in the homes in which they'd lived. For example, we read in 1 Samuel that after Samuel died, "all Israel assembled and mourned for him, and they buried him in his house at Ramah" (25:1).

Keeping their dead close was a physical sign that pointed to a deeper, more fundamental closeness. Pedersen writes:

> The family was rooted in its ancestors, and the blessing bestowed on the family could not be strengthened without the ancestors being included in the fellowship. At the Passover, it was the happiness of the forefathers, which was re-experienced. How the presence of the fathers found expression in other cult acts has not come down to us; probably a blessing was pronounced on them. That there was a living connection with the

departed results from the whole nature of the case.[1]

Pedersen then continues:

The relation between the living and the dead was mutual. The forefathers upheld the name by remaining with the descendants. And the family secured the right to their land and their blessing and that of the land by having their forefathers buried in the family soil.[2]

Ultimately, what you find here, in the ancient Israelites' attitude toward their dead, is something akin to the Communion of Saints. They recognized that a connection that can't be severed exists between the living and the dead. There is a relationship—again, a communion. It's not *the* Communion of Saints, but it's like it. It points to it. It's a natural sign of a supernatural reality that has yet to be revealed. But just because it hadn't been revealed to the ancient Israelites doesn't mean it wasn't believed—at least by some.

A Greater Hope

If all we had to go on were the first books of the Old Testament, this kind of natural communion between dead ancestors and their living descendants could make some sense of

[1] Johannes Pedersen, *Israel: Its Life and Culture* (Atlanta: Scholars Press, 1991), 2:476.

[2] Pedersen, *Israel*, 481.

what we see in Genesis, Exodus, and Joshua.

It would explain why Abraham went to such great lengths in Genesis 23 to purchase a burial site for his wife, Sarah, first refusing to accept the Hittites' offer of burying Sarah in one of their tombs and then refusing their offer of free land. Eventually, for the price of four hundred shekels, Abraham obtained a field with a cave, east of Mamre. There, his people, the descendants promised to him, could rest together, secure in their possession of the land.

The ancient Israelite belief in the tribal communion of the living and the dead would also make sense of why Jacob's dying wish was to be taken back to that cave and buried with his parents and grandparents, and why Joseph didn't just ask his children to carry his bones out of Egypt; he made them *swear an oath* that they would do so. Neither wanted to be buried in a foreign land, far from the family, living and dead, to which they belonged.

Again, if all we had were the books that make up the Pentateuch, it would be easy to chalk up the Patriarchs' reverence for the dead as a sort of ancestor worship. But we have more, starting with Hebrews 11, which tells us something about the faith of these men and women that the pages of the Pentateuch only hint at.

In Hebrews 11:9–10, we read of Abraham: "By faith he sojourned in the land of promise, as in a foreign land, living in tents with Isaac and Jacob, heirs with him of the same promise. For he looked forward to the city which has foundations, whose builder and maker is God."

We're also told, "By faith Abraham, when he was tested, offered up Isaac, and he who had received the promises was ready to offer up his only son . . . He considered that God was able to raise men even from the dead; hence, figuratively speaking, he did receive him back" (Heb 11:17, 19).

Likewise, we're told of his descendants:

> These all died in faith, not having received what was promised, but having seen it and greeted it from afar, and having acknowledged that they were strangers and exiles on the earth. For people who speak thus make it clear that they are seeking a homeland. If they had been thinking of that land from which they had gone out, they would have had opportunity to return. But as it is, they desire a better country, that is, a heavenly one. Therefore God is not ashamed to be called their God, for he has prepared for them a city. (Heb 11:13–16)

Again and again, the author of Hebrews drives home the point: Abraham knew. Isaac knew. Jacob knew. Joseph knew. The faithful Israelites knew. They knew there was more to life than this life—that there was a "better country." They knew that God had something better prepared for them—a "heavenly" homeland. They knew that their story wasn't over when their life was over—that their bodies, somehow, someway, were destined to be a part of that story, and so it mattered where and how those bodies were buried. When the day came to go to the "city" God had "prepared for them," they wanted to walk into that city together, as a family.

An Enduring Hope

Importantly, that hope in a city to come didn't die out with the Patriarchs.

It continued down through Israel's history, beginning with the Patriarchs' contemporary, Job, who pushed back against his friends' temptations to doubt, saying:

> For I know that my Redeemer lives, and at last he will stand upon the earth; and after my skin has been thus destroyed, then from my flesh I shall see God, whom I shall see on my side, and my eyes shall behold, and not another. (Job 19:25–27)

The Book of Daniel, which recounts events that took place during the time of the Babylonian exile, echoes that same hope. In Chapters 10–12, Daniel encounters "one in the likeness of the sons of men" (10:16), who reveals many things to him, including that the time will come when "Michael, the great prince who has charge of your people" (12:1) will arise. And at that point:

> There shall be a time of trouble, such as never has been since there was a nation till that time; but at that time your people shall be delivered, every one whose name shall be found written in the book. And many of those who sleep in the dust of the earth shall awake, some to everlasting life, and some to shame and everlasting contempt. And those who are wise shall shine like the brightness of the firmament; and those who turn many to righteousness,

like the stars for ever and ever. (Dan 12:1–3)

The faithful sons and daughters of Israel held on to that hope, right up through the Maccabean revolt in the second century before Jesus came. There, in 2 Maccabees, we see a mother of seven sons, urging on her sons to martyrdom, saying:

> The Creator of the world, who shaped the beginning of man and devised the origin of all things, will in his mercy give life and breath back to you again, since you now forget yourselves for the sake of his laws . . . Do not fear this butcher, but prove worthy of your brothers. Accept death, so that in God's mercy I may get you back again with your brothers. (2 Macc 7:23, 29)

Hebrews 11:35 later references that mother's faith, noting, "Women received their dead by resurrection. Some were tortured, refusing to accept release, that they might rise again to a better life."

How did that mother know about the resurrection? What did she know? How and what did any of the ancient Israelites know about rising "to a better life"? I don't know. Origen and St. Augustine and St. Thomas Aquinas all felt comfortable saying, "Yeah, they definitely believed in the Incarnation and the Trinity. They had explicit faith in the Christian mysteries."[3] But how that's possible is itself a mystery.

---

[3] For more on Aquinas's belief that the prophets and elders of Israel had an explicit faith in the Christian mysteries, see Fr. Matthew Lamb's introduction to St. Thomas's *Commentary on St. Paul's Epistle to the Ephesians*, trans. Matthew L. Lamb, O.C.S.O. (Albany, NY: Magi Books, 1966).

The truth is, we are too ignorant to discover why they weren't ignorant. We think we know what the Incarnation and the Trinity are, but when we get to heaven, I think we're going to look back and think that the parrot's words, "Polly want a cracker," shed as much light on these holy mysteries as the words we use to talk about them here and now. The realities to which these words point are infinitely greater, infinitely more beautiful, infinitely more astounding than the words we use to describe them. We have the words, and that's better than not having the words. But having the faith is better than having the words, and the words point to the faith that the Patriarchs and faithful Israelites clearly had before the Creed came.

That faith helped ancient Israel see what was on the horizon. It helped them grasp, however incompletely or imperfectly, the dignity of the body and the fate of the body in the life to come. It also shaped what they did with the body in this life and the importance they placed on what happened to those bodies—on where they rested and with whom they rested—in death.

The Patriarchs knew the Promised Land wasn't the ultimate Promised Land: It was just a signpost showing them the way to "the city which has foundations, whose builder and maker is God" (Heb 11:10). But there, in the first Promised Land, is where they wanted to be on the day they were invited, body and soul, into that heavenly city. The first Promised Land is where they received the gift of faith, and that's where they seemed to think the resurrection of the body should occur.

Not all of the Israelites had that faith, though. And even the ones who had it were tempted to lose it.

CHAPTER 4

PREPARING FOR A BETTER COUNTRY

At the dawn of creation, God filled the universe with signs that pointed to himself. The whole world was meant to be a type of catechesis, an instruction in who God is, what he does, and how he loves us.

It still is. Everywhere you look, there are natural analogies of his power, goodness, and love: the sun, the moon, the stars; the mountains, the oceans, the rivers; and especially, the man, the woman, and the child. Like the sun and the oceans, the human family reveals important truths about God. We are made in God's image, and how we care for each other, protect each other, and especially how we give life to each other—to new generations—teaches us something about God, whose nature is life-giving love.

This is good. The world, the family, what it has to teach us—it's all good. God created it to be good. But the good is not God, and in a fallen world, the danger always exists that we will confuse the two. That we will worship the sun instead of the one whose light the sun reflects. That we will worship the river instead of the one of whose power the river reminds us. That we will worship the earthly family instead of the divine family for which we were made.

This is demonic bait. The world is pointing to the world to come, but the devil doesn't want us to see that. Or, he doesn't want us to care. Satan wants to convince us that this world is all there is, that this life is enough.

But the natural world is passing, which means that to worship the natural is always to enter into a covenant with death. It's the deadliest form of worship. And yet, this is and was a temptation for fallen humanity. It was especially a temptation in a world where the fullness of truth had yet to be revealed, where God was only gradually filling in the blanks about who he is and what he has in store for us.

A Higher Purpose

The ancient Israelites knew this temptation—to worship creation and not the Creator—all too well. Despite what God had done for them, despite all the promises he made to Abraham, Isaac, and Jacob, the Patriarchs' descendants were just as susceptible as their neighbors were to nature worship. But they couldn't lead other nations to holiness if they were bowing down before golden cows or making offerings to river "gods." To make them into the people he needed them to be, God had to break them of this habit. He needed to teach them how to overcome this temptation and worship him alone. So, beginning in Exodus, you see God stepping in and using purity laws in an attempt to curtail the Israelites' proclivity to creation worship.

Just like we have the Old Testament and the New Testament, the Old Covenant and the New Covenant, we also, in a sense, have the Old Covenant of the Old Covenant and the New Covenant of the Old Covenant. That is, we have Genesis, and we have what comes after Genesis. There is a marked difference between the two, and Exodus is where that shift starts. In Exodus, we see a dramatic change in language and law as God slowly reveals more of his plan to Israel.

Take the word "holy." As the Old Testament scholar Robert Moberly notes, in Genesis the Hebrew word for "holy" appears only once. That's in Genesis 2:3 when we're told, "God blessed the seventh day and hallowed it." As soon as you get to Exodus, though, the word "holy" is everywhere.

It's at the burning bush: "Do not come near; put off your shoes from your feet, for the place on which you are standing is *holy* ground" (Exod 3:5).

It's at Mount Sinai: "And you shall be to me a kingdom of priests and a *holy* nation" (Exod 19:6).

It's in the instructions for the new tabernacle: "And you shall hang the veil from the clasps, and bring the ark of the testimony in thither within the veil; and the veil shall separate for you the *holy* place from the most *holy*" (Exod 26:33).

In Exodus alone, the world "holy" occurs more than fifty times. What changed? It's simple: time. What we see here is a pedagogical process, where God is slowly revealing himself over time, helping Israel to grow up, to mature in faith, and to let go of the natural so that they are ready to receive the supernatural. Essentially, in Exodus he starts laying out a higher calling for his people, a *holy* calling, a calling to be more distinctly set apart from the nations around them so that, eventually, they can lead those nations to him.

A Divine Pedagogy

One of the first steps in that process is breaking Israel from any tendency to ancestor worship and helping the Israelites to see what death really is.

This is why specific mourning rites are forbidden in Leviticus and Deuteronomy, such as the shaving of the head and the gashing of the skin (Lev 19:27, 21:5; Deut 14:1). Both rites were practiced among the Canaanites, who saw those acts as a way of making sacrifices to and communing with the dead.

For similar reasons, the Israelites are forbidden from offering tithes to the dead, such as wheat or animal products (Deut 26:14). Throughout the ancient world, people commonly made offerings to the dead or buried the dead with wealth and food. But Israel was not to be like its neighbors.

Likewise, in Numbers 19:11 we read, "He who touches the dead body of any person shall be unclean seven days." Numbers then goes on to outline an elaborate cleansing ritual, not only for those who touch the dead but also for anyone who even goes into the tent of someone who died.

Why would God issue such laws? Because the Israelites were going to catch cooties from the dead body? Because the body isn't hygienic?

No. Because God wanted Israel to understand that physical death is a sign of spiritual death. It's a sign of what sin does to the soul. And sin is catching. It's as contagious as any disease and as deadly as any disease. More deadly, actually.

We see this even more explicitly in Ezekiel 37 when God has Ezekiel preach to a valley of dead bones. The bones are a symbol of Israel. They are dead and defiled. And the defilement of their physical condition is a sign of the defilement of their spiritual condition. They had forgotten God, forgotten his ways, and lost the hope he had promised them. Through that forgetting, they defiled their souls. "Behold, they say, 'Our bones are dried up, and our hope is lost; we are clean cut off'" (Ezek 37:11).

Telling the Israelites that touching the dead defiles them is a pedagogical lesson to help the Israelites learn to detest sin. The same goes for the prohibition on touching a leper. God doesn't primarily care about skin purity. He cares about soul purity. And leprosy in the Bible is a sign of sin. It does to a person's body what breaking God's law does to the soul. In a way, God telling Israel that touching the dead or the lepers makes them unclean is like my mom washing my mouth out with soap the first time she caught me lying. She tried to teach me a lesson internally by applying the punishment externally.

Walking the Line

Throughout the Old Testament, in the practices of ancient Israel, we can plainly see that even among those who don't know about the resurrection to come or believe in the resurrection to come, there is still reverence for the body. In a state of pure nature, with natural religion, there is natural communion, and graves are the natural places for natural religious practices to take place.

God, however, wants Israel to reverence the dead, not worship the dead. He wants them to imitate their holy ancestors, not idolize them. He doesn't want them to be like their neighbors and try to commune with the dead through mediums and witchcraft. He wants them to have real communion with the dead in the communion of the saints.

So, God has to break his people of some of those natural tendencies. He has to help them see that those natural practices and that natural communion are just signposts showing the way to something much more glorious and much more powerful than they can imagine.

What God never attempts to do, though, is break the Israelites of their natural reverence for the body. So, from Exodus on we see Israel walk this fine line where touching a dead body defiles but not burying a body is a curse. To approach the dead, touch the dead, or be near the dead brings no special blessing to the Israelites. Nothing is to be gained from the body. And yet, it still must be treated with reverence. It must be buried. It must be mourned.

We see this in 2 Samuel 21, when Saul's granddaughter, Rizpah, lived outside and kept watch over her dead sons, whom the Gibeonites had killed and then left on a mountain to be eaten by the birds. Rather than see her boys' bodies defiled in such a way, Rizpah "took sackcloth, and spread it for herself on the rock, from the beginning of harvest until rain fell upon them from the heavens; and she did not allow the birds of the air to come upon them by day, or the beasts of the field by night" (21:10). Eventually, her piety aroused David's sympathy, and he had the bodies recovered and buried.

We also see similar piety, most strikingly, in the Book of Tobit.

A Faithful Israelite

The Bible tells us that during the Assyrian exile, a faithful Israelite named Tobit managed to gain the favor of the king and become the buyer of provisions for the palace. That was a position of great honor for anyone, but especially for an Israelite, an outsider. Nevertheless, Tobit repeatedly risked his life, fortune, and position because he insisted on secretly burying the Israelites who were slain and cast over the city walls.

> I would give my bread to the hungry and my clothing to the naked; and if I saw any one of my people dead and thrown out behind the wall of Nineveh, I would bury him. And if Sennacherib the king put to death any who came fleeing from Judea, I buried them secretly. For in his anger he put many to death. When the bodies were sought by the king, they were not found. (Tob 1:17–18)

Eventually, Tobit is found out and flees, losing everything, save for his wife and son, in the process. Tobit accepts that punishment. He knew that was the risk from the beginning. But he took it anyway. For us, it's hard to understand why he would do such a thing. In some ways, it's like he was majoring in the minors. Yes, he wanted to be faithful. But wasn't it enough for him to keep the Sabbath, eat kosher, light some candles, and wait to worry about the dead until it was legal to worry about the dead?

Not for Tobit. He understood this was a test of faith, not just an expression of faith. It wasn't just about natural piety; it was about supernatural hope.

He proclaims that hope in Tobit 13, exclaiming a song of praise that begins:

> Blessed is God who lives for ever,
> and blessed is his kingdom.
> For he afflicts, and he shows mercy;
> he leads down to Hades, and brings up again,
> and there is no one who can escape his hand.
> (Tob 13:1–2)

Note: Tobit says that God "brings up again" those who went down to Hades, that is, to the land of the dead. Like Abraham, Isaac, and Jacob; like Joseph, Job, and Daniel; like the mother from 2 Maccabees; and like all the faithful remnant of humanity who came before him and will come after him, Tobit believes God will raise the dead—not just spiritually, but physically. After all, if the resurrection were just going to be spiritual, what happened to bodies in death wouldn't matter. But with a physical resurrection, bodies matter. What happens to bodies matters. How bodies are buried matters.

And so, as Tobit understands it, until the day resurrection comes, the dead must be buried with reverence, so their bodies can wait for that resurrection in peace. Fittingly, Tobit's last instructions to his son reference his burial: "Bury me properly, and your mother with me" (Tob 14:10).

His son, Tobias, complies. We're told, "Tobias gave him a magnificent funeral. And when Anna died he buried her with his father" (Tob 14:11–12).

In a way, the whole Book of Tobit is one long reminder about how Israel is to treat the dead. Tobit risked everything to care for the bodies of those who had passed. Because of that, God blessed him, sending the Angel Raphael to travel with his son Tobias and find him a bride, save him from a demon, bring him home safely, and then cure Tobit's own blindness. Tobit reverenced the dead, and so God blessed Tobit. That's the message.

Importantly, this was before Jesus's Resurrection, before humanity knew exactly what God planned to do with the body. This was in the Old Testament, when the resurrection was just the subtext, a promise hinted at but not explained, bubbling beneath the surface of all the other events of salvation history. With Jesus's coming, however, the subtext became the text. The promise hinted at became the promise explained. And the idea bubbling beneath the surface burst into the open, revealing itself to be the very heart of Jesus's mission and the end goal of salvation history.

CHAPTER 5

HOPE TO RISE

W hen I was in high school, one of my favorite books was *Systematic Theology* by Louis Berkhof, a Dutch Reformed theologian. Like most books I read at the time, this book covered the Resurrection of Jesus Christ in two to three pages. It didn't talk about what the Resurrection had to do with our salvation, though. It just discussed the Resurrection from an apologetics standpoint. It focused on proving the Resurrection as a historical fact—that the stone was rolled away, the tomb was empty, and the body was raised. But why any of that really mattered? That didn't come into play.

I continued to think of the Resurrection in those terms— as a historical fact in need of proving—for some time. But after I started reading the Church Fathers, I began to see how much more there was to the Resurrection. I realized that, in some ways, to the first Apostles and Evangelists the Resurrection didn't simply matter; it was *all* that mattered. The Resurrection, more than anything else, was what they preached and wrote about. The Resurrection—not Jesus's

Sermon on the Mount or his run-ins with the Pharisees—was what they proclaimed.

Consider the very first sermon ever preached by the Church: Peter's proclamation of the Gospel in Jerusalem following the descent of the Holy Spirit on Pentecost. In Acts 2, after calling the crowd to attention, Peter begins by quoting the prophet Joel, explaining why the Apostles could suddenly speak in different languages. Next, in exactly one sentence, he summarizes Jesus's life and ministry. After that, again in one sentence, he covers the Paschal Mystery.

Then, in Acts 2:24, he begins talking about Jesus's Resurrection, announcing that "God raised him up, having loosed the pangs of death, because it was not possible for him to be held by it." Peter continues talking about the Resurrection, for the next twelve verses, the remainder of his sermon. He preaches about how God raised Jesus from the dead, how King David foresaw the Resurrection, how the Apostles were witnesses to the Resurrection, and how the resurrected Christ now sits at the right hand of the Father. From (almost) first to last, the entirety of Peter's preaching is about the Resurrection.

That's not just true of Peter's first sermon, though. It's also true of the Gospels, Acts, and the Epistles. Again and again, the writers circle back to Christ's Resurrection. Not just the fact of it, but what it accomplishes: our resurrection.

For years, I couldn't see that. Then, one day, I couldn't see anything but that. It's like the magic eye art that was so popular in the 1990s. At first glance, those computer-generated prints look like nothing more than a random collection of geographic shapes and colors. But the more you look at them, the more your vision shifts until finally it discovers the image hidden within. After that, you can't unsee the image. You can't go back to just seeing shapes and colors.

That's what it's like when you start seeing the thread of the Resurrection running through Sacred Scripture. You can't unsee it. You can't go back to just thinking of the Resurrection as a historical fact that needs to be proved. You think of it, instead, as the very heart of Jesus's mission and, as St. Athanasius put it, "The supreme object of His coming, was to bring about the resurrection of the body."[1]

Jesus's Resurrection

Jesus was born into a people and culture where belief in the resurrection of the dead was no longer assumed but rather disputed. One group of religious authorities—the Pharisees—pointed back to the testimony of the ancient Israelites and prophets in the Scripture and argued for some kind of resurrection (whether bodily or not is a question still debated by scholars). Another group of religious authorities—the Sadducees—denied the whole idea of the resurrection. From the first moments of his public ministry, no one who heard Jesus preach doubted which side of the question he took.

Jesus began talking about the resurrection of one particular body—his own—from the first days of his public ministry. In John 2, almost immediately after performing his first public miracle in Cana, Jesus goes to Jerusalem and hints

[1] Athanasius, *On the Incarnation*, 52.

at his Resurrection for the first time, telling the Jewish authorities, "Destroy this temple, and in three days I will raise it up" (John 2:19). He wasn't talking about the actual temple of stones, though. As John recognizes, "he spoke of the temple of his body" (John 2:21).

Months passed, and Jesus stops hinting about what the Father has in store for him and begins explaining it directly to his Apostles:

> From that time Jesus began to show his disciples that he must go to Jerusalem and suffer many things from the elders and chief priests and scribes, and be killed, and on the third day be raised. (Matt 16:21)

Jesus mentions his Resurrection again after the Transfiguration on Mt. Tabor, warning Peter, James, and John, "Tell no one the vision, until the Son of man is raised from the dead" (Matt 17:9).

Then, on the way to Jerusalem in the days leading up to his Passion, he makes it clear what lies ahead:

> Behold, we are going up to Jerusalem; and the Son of man will be delivered to the chief priests and scribes, and they will condemn him to death, and deliver him to the Gentiles to be mocked and scourged and crucified, and he will be raised on the third day. (Matt 20:18–19)

Finally, on the night before his death, he again tells his Apostles, "But after I am raised up, I will go before you to Galilee" (Matt 26:32).

Throughout all four Gospels, Jesus leaves little room for doubt: He is the one in whom Job, so many thousands of years before, had professed his faith. He is the redeemer who lives. He also is the one in whom Abraham, Isaac, and Jacob hoped. "Your father Abraham rejoiced that he was to see my day," Jesus tells the Jews. "He saw it and was glad" (John 8:56).

But it's not Jesus's own Resurrection about which he talks the most. The resurrection that he is far more concerned with is ours.

Our Resurrection

Looking back on Jesus's three years of public preaching, it's easy to miss the forest for the trees and think that the point of his teaching was to give humanity a code of conduct, a way to live in the world. And Jesus did give us that.

He told us to "love the Lord your God with all your heart, and with all your soul, and with all your mind," to "love your neighbor as yourself," and "love one another as I have loved you" (Matt 22:37, 39; John 15:12). He also told us to turn the other cheek in a dispute, to give to the poor, and to pray for those who persecute us. He explained who our neighbor was—every man—and that we have a responsibility to every man, that indeed whenever we feed the hungry, clothe the naked, give shelter to the homeless, or visit the imprisoned, we are doing all those things to and for him. Above all, Jesus urged us to not worry or be anxious, to pray to God as Our Father, and to look for the coming of the kingdom of God.

Jesus's aim in giving us those teachings wasn't to create some kind of earthly paradise. Nor was our reward for heeding them the privilege of living a nice, comfortable earthly life. The goal of it all was heaven. It was eternal life. It was our resurrection.

"If you would enter life," he tells one would-be follower, "keep the commandments" (Matt 19:17). Later, when explaining the Kingdom of Heaven in Matthew 25, he warns that those who ignore the hungry, the thirsty, the stranger, the naked, the sick, and the imprisoned will "go away into eternal punishment," while the righteous—those who care for the needy instead of ignoring them—will go "into eternal life" (Matt 25:34–46).

Jesus also promises his Apostles that their reward for leaving "house or wife or brothers or parents or children, for the sake of the kingdom of God" will be "manifold more in this time, and in the age to come eternal life" (Luke 18:29–30). And in the Gospel of John he plainly states to Martha: "I am the resurrection and the life; he who believes in me, though he die, yet shall he live" (11:25).

Moreover, unlike the debate over what the Pharisees believed about the resurrection—whether it would be bodily or only spiritual—Jesus's words affirm the reality of a physical resurrection. To one large crowd he announced, "For this is the will of my Father, that every one who sees the Son and believes in him should have eternal life; and I will raise him up at the last day" (John 6:40).

To another group of Jews he said, "Do not marvel at this; for the hour is coming when all who are in the tombs will hear his voice and come forth, those who have done good, to the resurrection of life, and those who have done evil, to the resurrection of judgment" (John 5:28–29).

Two Resurrections

If you read closely, you can see that Jesus was talking about more than one kind of resurrection. Remember there is life (*bios*) and life (*zoe*). There is also spiritual death and physical death. Jesus's words address both kinds of life and both kinds of death.

In John 5:28, Jesus explicitly affirms the physical resurrection of the dead, saying "the hour is coming when all who are in the tombs will hear his voice and come forth." But just three verses earlier, in John 5:25, Jesus talks about a different kind of resurrection: "Truly, truly, I say to you, the hour is coming, and now is, when the dead will hear the voice of the Son of God, and those who hear will live."

"The hour is coming and *now is*," meaning, man doesn't have to wait for his physical death to experience resurrection. The dead can hear his voice *now*. The dead can live *now*. But how?

He tells us how in both John 5:25 and in John 5:24: "He who hears my word and believes him who sent me, has eternal life." Note: *has* eternal life. Not "will have." *Has*. There is only one kind of eternal life that can be had now, in this life, in this moment, and that is *zoe*—divine life, supernatural life, the life that Adam and Eve had in the beginning and then lost through original sin.

But that raises another question: Who are the dead who need to hear his word and believe *now*? They're the zombies we talked about in Chapter 1—the walking dead, the living dead, those who are physically alive but dead in sin, who lack the life of God—sanctifying grace—in their souls. These are the men and women who Jesus tells us in John 3 must be "born anew" of "water and the Spirit" (3:3, 5).

Jesus came to give us both kinds of life, *bios* and *zoe*. He came to overcome both kinds of death, spiritual and physical. The one, however, precedes the other. You are resurrected spiritually first so that even when you die physically, you can be resurrected physically later on the last day. It's like a slinky going down the stairs, with one end always lagging behind the other. Similarly, when it comes to resurrection, the body has to catch up to the soul.

John alludes to this, talking about a "first resurrection" in the Book of Revelation: "Blessed and holy is he who shares in the first resurrection! Over such the second death has no power, but they shall be priests of God and of Christ, and they shall reign with him a thousand years" (20:6).

So, over the person who participates in the "first resurrection," death has no power—not the first death, which is the physical death of the body, and not the second death, which is the Final Judgment. Just a few sentences later, John goes on to describe the second resurrection of the just and the second death of the unjust:

> And I saw the dead, great and small, standing before the throne, and books were opened. Also another book was opened, which is the book of life. And the dead were judged by what was written in the books, by what they had done. And the sea gave up the dead in it, Death and Hades gave up the dead in them, and all were judged by what they had done.

Then Death and Hades were thrown into the lake of fire. This is the second death, the lake of fire; and if any one's name was not found written in the book of life, he was thrown into the lake of fire. (Rev 20:12–15)

To Jesus's listeners, all this talk about resurrection made no sense. He said the most outrageous things: "He who eats my flesh and drinks my blood has eternal life, and I will raise him up at the last day" (John 6:54); "I am the light of the world; he who follows me will not walk in darkness, but will have the light of life" (John 8:12); "Truly, truly, I say to you, if any one keeps my word, he will never see death" (John 8:51).

"Who is this guy?" his listeners wondered. "Is he crazy to make such claims? Or possessed?"

The Jews said to him, "Now we know that you have a demon. Abraham died, as did the prophets; and you say, 'If any one keeps my word, he will never taste death.' Are you greater than our father Abraham, who died? And the prophets died! Who do you claim to be?" (John 8:52–53)

Jesus's answer affirms the resurrection hope of the Old Testament: "Your father Abraham rejoiced that he was to see my day; he saw it and was glad" (John 8:56). In other words, Jesus *is* the one come to fulfill the Old Covenant. Jesus *is* the one come to make the long hoped-for resurrection possible and deliver people from the fear of death.

But how will he do that? How can he do that?

Jesus's miracles, worked during his earthly life, give us part of the answer.

Powers That Come Forth

In the *Catechism of the Catholic Church*, we're told that "sacraments are 'powers that come forth' from the Body of Christ, which is ever-living and life-giving" (CCC 1116). These sacraments are the means by which God "resurrects us" in this life. Baptism restores divine life to our souls. The Eucharist nourishes that life. Confession replenishes it. Confirmation, Marriage, and Holy Orders strengthen it. And the Anointing of the Sick stirs up the divine life within us to heal our bodies and prepare our souls for eternal life.

Today, as the Catechism says, the graces of all these sacraments come to us from the Body of Christ on earth, the Church. But before there was the Body of Christ, there was *the* body of Christ. Prior to the institution of the sacraments, Jesus is *the* sacrament. So, in the Gospels, it's his actual physical body from which "powers . . . come forth." In his lifetime, those powers did to people's bodies what the sacraments have done to people's souls ever since.

Nowhere is this stated more explicitly than in Luke 8, when a hemorrhaging woman presses up against Jesus in the crowds and touches his garments, believing that all she needed to be healed was physical contact with Jesus.

She was right. Scripture tells us, "immediately her flow of blood ceased" (Luke 8:44). But her touch didn't go unnoticed. Despite all the people pushing against him, Jesus knew one touch was different. "Some one touched me; for

I perceive that power has gone forth from me," he tells his Apostles (Luke 8:46).

We see that same power at work throughout the Gospels, with Jesus's word and touch accomplishing in people's bodies what the sacraments now accomplish in our souls.

For example, it's Jesus's word and touch that restore physical life to the dead, much as Baptism restores physical life to our souls. In Luke 8:54–55, he takes the hand of a dead child, speaks to her, and "her spirit returned, and she got up at once." Then, in John 11:43–44, it's his voice that brings Lazarus back from the dead: "He cried with a loud voice, 'Lazarus, come out.' The dead man came out, his hands and feet bound with bandages, and his face wrapped with a cloth."

It's also Jesus's word and touch that nourish life—that feed people's bodies and strengthen them, like the Eucharist feeds the divine life in souls and like Confirmation strengthens that life. First on a plain, then on a mountaintop, Jesus prays a blessing over a handful of fish and a few loaves of bread, breaks that bread with his hands, and suddenly that paltry amount of food becomes enough to feed a multitude, five thousand the first time, four thousand the second time (Matt 14:17–22; 15:34–38).

And it's Jesus's word and touch that heal bodies, much like the sacraments of Confession and the Anointing of the Sick heal us in body and soul. He touches or spits on the eyes of the blind, and their sight is restored (Matt 20:34; Mark 8:23–25; John 9:6). He puts his fingers into the ears of the deaf and his spit on the tongue of the mute, says one word, *Eph'phatha* ("Be opened"), and hearing and speech follow (Mark 7:34–35). He cures the sick simply by telling them to be cured: "Rise, take up your pallet, and walk" (John 5:8). And he makes the lame walk by doing the same: "I say to you, rise, take up your pallet and go home" (Mark 2:11). Sins are also forgiven at his word: "And when Jesus saw their faith, he said to the paralytic, 'My son, your sins are forgiven'" (Mark 2:5).

Again, throughout the Gospels, Jesus's body does to our bodies what the sacraments do to our souls. Jesus's body heals bodies. Jesus's body teaches bodies. Jesus's body feeds bodies. Jesus's body raises bodies from the dead. Throughout his public ministry, powers go forth from his body, restoring people to the fullness of natural life.

But the restoration of natural life isn't enough. Jesus came for so much more than that. And the healings he works on earth both foreshadow the "more" and prove that more is possible. That is, they foreshadow the resurrection to come and prove that Jesus means what he says when he promises that all will rise again with him on the last day.

When people touch him and are healed or when he touches them and they are healed, Jesus demonstrates for all who have eyes to see that he holds power over death. All the physical forms of death—death of the eyes to blindness, death of the ears to deafness, death of the limbs to paralysis, death of the skin to leprosy, and even the death of the entire person to illness—are overcome by the Incarnate one over the course of his ministry.

With every healing, Jesus shows people that they don't have to be afraid of death. They don't have to be slaves to the anxiety that grips them when they think of the grave and that leads them to sin. That's what Hebrews 2:15 tells us: Jesus came to "deliver all those who through fear of death were subject to lifelong bondage." Jesus's miracles were a testimony to the truth of his words. Through his preaching, Jesus assured us of the fact of our resurrection, and his miracles testified to his ability to make our body like his through resurrection.

But neither his preaching nor his miracles make our resurrection possible.

So, what does?

CHAPTER 6

✠

THE EUCHARIST AND THE RESURRECTION OF THE BODY

All those years ago, when I was a teenager who thought of Jesus's Resurrection as a historical event, demonstrably proven true by details like the empty tomb and eyewitnesses, I wasn't wrong. It is a historical event. But it's not *just* a historical event. Nor is it a historical event in the same way that the Battle of Waterloo or the moon landing are historical events. It's a historical event, *and* it's a miracle. It involves God's direct intervention in human history, accomplishing something through grace that could never otherwise be accomplished through nature.

But Jesus's Resurrection isn't just a miracle either. It's the fulfillment of prophecy. Jesus's Resurrection fulfills his own prophecies and the prophecies of the Old Testament.

It doesn't end there, though, because Jesus's Resurrection doesn't just fulfill prophecies; it fulfills the *entirety* of the Old Testament. Jesus's Resurrection fulfills God's covenant with Israel and unveils a New Covenant with all the world.

Jesus's Resurrection likewise is a vindication of his innocence. It demonstrates to the Pharisees, Sadducees, and Roman soldiers that he was indeed who he said he was: the Son of God, the Messiah, the great "I Am."

But the Resurrection isn't simply Jesus coming back from the dead to say, "I told you so." Nor is it the resuscitation of a corpse like you see with Lazarus in John 11. Lazarus came back to life only to die again. That's not what Jesus did. Jesus came back to life never to die again. Jesus came back to life with a body incapable of death, a body transfigured and glorified, a body that bore the wounds of his crucifixion but that could also pass through walls and be in Emmaus one second, then in Jerusalem the next.

In that sense, the Resurrection is further proof of Jesus's divinity. But it's still more than that. It's more than everything else the Resurrection was. The Resurrection is the divinization of his humanity. It's the created passing into the uncreated, the temporal entering into the eternal. And *that* is what opens the door for our own resurrection, our own transfiguration and glorification.

It does that, though, not as a stand-alone event but as part of what the Church calls the "Paschal Mystery."

Good Friday to Holy Sunday

For a long time, even as a Catholic, I thought of the story of our salvation as a tale in two parts: Jesus's death and Jesus's Resurrection. On the cross, Jesus offered himself as a sacrifice to atone for our sins. Then, on Easter Sunday, he rose from the dead to bring about our justification—to apply his righteousness to us.

This isn't wrong. St. Paul explicitly states it in Romans 4:25, noting that Jesus was "put to death for our trespasses and raised for our justification." The *Catechism of the Catholic Church* explains it even more fully, saying:

> The Paschal Mystery has two aspects: by his death, Christ liberates us from sin; by his Resurrection, he opens for us the way to a new life. This new life is above all justification that reinstates us in God's grace . . . Justification consists in both victory over the death caused by sin and a new participation in grace. (cf. Eph 2:4–5; 1 Pet 1:3) (CCC 654)

On Good Friday, God the Son gave God the Father the one thing the Father had always wanted from humanity: filial love. On the cross, Jesus Christ, who in the Incarnation had taken on human flesh and a human nature, offered himself to God in loving obedience. He didn't allow himself to be beaten and tortured and hung on a cross simply out of a sense of duty or fear of God's wrath. He said, "Thy will be done," because of love. He sacrificed himself because he loved the Father, trusted the Father, and knew whatever the Father asked of him was likewise asked in love—perfect love.

Through that loving "yes," Jesus perfectly atoned for humanity's transgressions. He paid the debt we could not pay. It wasn't a debt he owed, but because he had joined himself to us in the Incarnation, becoming man, he could offer the payment on our behalf.

Jesus's death, however, wasn't just his own. The great twentieth-century theologian F. X. Durrwell writes:

> Jesus' death, then, is an activity of limitless scope. It is an immense cosmic river which drains humanity and is capable of embracing within its waves all beings-for-death, in other words, all men and women, and to make of them in their death beings who are born of God . . . In Jesus, death shines with an incomparable brilliance. It is divine. It is the Trinitarian mystery of the one who, in the infinite power of the Holy Spirit, is carried to the Father, to the extent that he is one with him. And that death is universal salvation. JESUS DIES THE DEATH OF ALL, realizing in his death, the death of each one.[1]

Jesus died the death of all. When he died on the cross, he somehow made it possible for all who believed in him to die as well.

Then, on Easter Sunday, Jesus rose again. And in that rising, Jesus defeated death's power over humanity. Just as all believers die in the death of Christ's body, so can all rise again in the Resurrection of his body: "For as in Adam all die, so also in Christ shall all be made alive" (1 Cor 15:22). The same brotherhood of mankind that enabled him to atone for the sins of humanity also enabled him to forever change the meaning of death for humanity. St. Athanasius explains:

---

[1] F. X. Durrwell, *Christ, Humankind and Death*, trans. Alphonsus Thomas, C.Ss.R. (Sherbrooke, Québec: Médiaspaul, 1999), 41. Emphasis in original.

> For the solidarity of mankind is such that, by virtue of the Word's indwelling in a single human body, the corruption with death has lost its power over all. You know how it is when some great king enters a large city and dwells in one of its houses; because of his dwelling in a single house, the whole city is honored, and enemies and robbers cease to molest it. Even so it is with the King of all; He has come into our country and dwelt in one body amidst the many, and in consequence the designs of the enemy against mankind have been foiled, and the corruption of death, which formerly held them in its power, has simply ceased to be.[2]

The grave could not hold Jesus Christ. Because of that, it cannot hold all those united to him.

Moreover, because the Resurrection was so much more than the resuscitation of Jesus's dead body—because it was, in fact, the glorification of his humanity—the Resurrection makes possible the glorification of all humanity. It offers all those who die in Christ the promise of rising like Christ: "For if we have been united with him in a death like his, we shall certainly be united with him in a resurrection like his" (Rom 6:5).

What does a "resurrection like his" mean, though?

Remember, Jesus's Resurrection isn't simply Jesus coming back to life. It's Jesus coming back to a new life in a glorified body. His glorified body bears the wounds of his suffering and death but cannot die. His glorified body can

---

[2]   Athanasius, *On the Incarnation,* 35.

be recognizable to his closest friends (and is recognizable when he appears to them in the Upper Room) but also can be unrecognizable as well (Mary Magdalene, the disciples on the road to Emmaus, and the Apostles at the beach all fail to recognize Jesus at once). And his glorified body can be held and touched, can eat and drink and cook, but also isn't bound by the normal rules of time and space.

The resurrected Christ is not a ghost or a spirit, but he also isn't a body like he once was. He has been resurrected to a new life, in a new kind of body, and that is the kind of resurrection, that is the kind of body that is promised to us, one that is "sown in dishonor . . . raised in glory . . . sown in weakness . . . raised in power . . . sown a physical body . . . raised a spiritual body" (1 Cor 15:43–44).

Holy Thursday

That's the story in two parts: Jesus dying and rising again; Jesus atoning for our trespasses and justifying us so that we might live forever as the adopted children of God. But, as I've come to see, there's more to the story, more to the Paschal Mystery, than just Good Friday and Easter Sunday. There's also Holy Thursday.

The night before he died, Jesus gathered in a room with his Apostles to celebrate the Passover feast—the feast that recalled the angel of death "passing over" all the Israelites who partook of the first Passover feast in Egypt. On Holy Thursday, though, Jesus wasn't celebrating the Passover one last time. He was fulfilling it and instituting a new Passover feast.

From the very first, the Passover was never just a meal. It was always part of a sacrifice. The lamb was slain and then eaten. But that lamb also wasn't just a lamb, and sacrificing it couldn't really spare the Israelites from death. The Israelites who were spared from death on the first Passover, in Egypt, still eventually died. The Israelites who partook of the Passover meal in every year that followed still died. Accordingly, the lamb and the Passover meal were both what biblical scholars call "types"; they were foreshadowings of deeper truths and deeper realities yet to be revealed. They foreshadowed the true Lamb of God who would take away death from the world and the true Passover feast that would give life to the world.

The true Lamb of God was Jesus Christ, who in that room on Holy Thursday, in the midst of the old Passover liturgy, broke bread and, offering it to his disciples said, "This is my Body, which will be given up for you."[3] Then, at the end of the liturgy, he held up what was typically considered the third cup of blessing and announced, "This is the chalice of my Blood, the Blood of the new and eternal covenant, which will be poured out for you and for many."[4]

It's those words, spoken at that meal, which make what happened a few hours later on Calvary a sacrifice. Without them, Jesus's death isn't a sacrifice; it's just an execution—the bloody, violent taking of an innocent man's life. But with those words, Jesus's death is the sacrifice of the true paschal lamb. It's Jesus as our new and eternal high priest

---

[3]   *The Roman Missal*, trans. The International Commission on English in the Liturgy, 3rd typical ed. (Washington, DC: United States Conference of Catholic Bishops, 2011), no. 119.

[4]   *The Roman Missal*, no. 120.

offering the New Covenant Passover Sacrifice. It's the reality to which all those Passover sacrifices, through all those long centuries, pointed.

The events of Holy Thursday spill over to Good Friday, transforming what happens on the cross from execution to saving sacrifice. But they don't stop there. They also spill over to Easter Sunday, making Jesus's resurrected, glorified, deified humanity communicable and distributable and edible to all who partake in the New Covenant Passover Sacrifice: the Eucharist.

The Living Bread

Well before he walked up the steep road to Calvary, Jesus told his listeners how our resurrection would take place: "I am the living bread which came down from heaven; if any one eats of this bread, he will live for ever" (John 6:51).

And what is this bread? Jesus tells us in the very same line: "The bread which I shall give for the life of the world is my flesh" (John 6:51).

Not surprisingly, his Jewish listeners find this plan for resurrection decidedly unkosher. "How can this man give us his flesh to eat?" they ask (John 6:52).

So, Jesus gets even more specific:

> Truly, truly, I say to you, unless you eat the flesh of
> the Son of man and drink his blood, you have no life
> in you; he who eats my flesh and drinks my blood
> has eternal life, and I will raise him up at the last
> day. For my flesh is food indeed, and my blood is

drink indeed. He who eats my flesh and drinks my blood abides in me, and I in him. (John 6:53–56)

Later, on Holy Thursday, in the Upper Room, he shows us how this is possible, holding up first the bread and then the cup, saying, "This is my body . . . This is the cup of my blood," and commanding the Twelve to "do this in memory of me."[5] In the original Greek of Luke's Gospel, the word we translate as "memory" is *anamnesis,* which means so much more than simply "remembering." It suggests a way of recalling past events that effectively makes the past present. In other words, you're not repeating the action of the past; you're entering into that very same action.

So, when Jesus tells the Apostles to "do this in memory of me," he is commanding them to offer in time what he would offer the next day on Calvary and offer eternally in heaven. They're not repeating the sacrifice. They can't. You can't repeat what never ends. They're making present Jesus Christ's own perpetual offering of himself.

They're also enabling us to participate in the New Passover Sacrifice.

In the Eucharist, we consume the Lamb of God as the Israelites consumed the sacrificial lamb. That Lamb is the resurrected Christ. At every Mass, we consume Jesus's resurrected, glorified body under the appearance of bread and wine. We eat the flesh and drink the blood of the God who became man, died, and rose again. The body that we eat is the same body that hung on the cross, lay in the tomb, and then rose from the dead. That body is also the same

---

[5] *The Roman Missal,* nos. 119–120.

body that passed through walls, that could be in Emmaus one minute and Jerusalem the next, and then ascended into heaven to sit at the right hand of the Father.

God didn't raise Jesus from the dead, though, and then welcome him back into heaven on Ascension Thursday in order to keep him tucked away behind some heavenly throne, safe from all the evil mortal men can do. Nor did Jesus ascend into heaven to protect himself or hide from the world in his Father's sanctuary. If anything, Jesus's Ascension makes him the sanctuary. It makes him the place of refuge for all who believe in him. It also makes him the eternal high priest, who can forever offer himself, forever give himself, forever communicate himself to us.

Holy Communion

Before Jesus's Passion, death, and Resurrection he was the King of Kings. Even before the Incarnation, he was the King of Kings. Jesus was always the Lord of Creation, the true King that earthly kings could only image in part. But he was not the eternal high priest. It's the sacrifice instituted on Holy Thursday, offered on Good Friday, and perpetuated forever after Jesus's Resurrection and Ascension that makes him a royal high priest.

As our high priest, Jesus is now always offering himself. And in the Mass, as members of his body, adopted into the family of God through Baptism, we are always receiving him. That reception makes possible what Jesus long ago promised: that whoever ate his flesh and drank his blood would not perish but have eternal life. In Holy Communion, he enters into our mortal bodies so that we, in turn, can enter into his immortal, glorified body.

Reflecting on how this is possible, Joseph Ratzinger (Pope Benedict XVI) writes:

> Hence Communion means that the seemingly uncrossable frontier of my "I" is left wide open and can be so because Jesus has first allowed himself to be opened completely, has taken us all into himself and has put himself totally into our hands. Hence, Communion means the fusion of existences; just as in the taking of nourishment the body assimilates foreign matter to itself, and is thereby enabled to live, in the same way my "I" is assimilated to that of Jesus, it is made similar to him in an exchange that increasingly breaks through the lines of division.[6]

When we eat a hamburger or pizza or an apple, that hamburger or pizza or apple becomes part of us. We assimilate it into our bodies. But when we consume the Body and Blood of Jesus in Holy Communion, the exact opposite happens. Instead of us assimilating Jesus into our bodies, he assimilates us into his body. He doesn't become part of our body. We become part of his body.

It is through this mysterious exchange of grace that the Eucharist becomes the instrumental cause of our resurrection. It works in our souls as both food and medicine, feeding us with God's life, healing our souls of the effects

---

[6] Joseph Ratzinger, *Called to Communion: Understanding the Church Today*, trans. Adrian Walker (San Francisco: Ignatius Press, 1996), 37.

of venial sin, and making us, day by day, into saints. It is the Eucharist that nourishes our souls, strengthens our commitment to living lives of grace, and unites us to our fellow believers, forming us corporately into the Body of Christ. Lastly, it is the Eucharist that imbues our mortal bodies with the capacity to be divinized and glorified and resurrected in the Body of Christ. As the Catechism puts it, the Eucharist is "the seed of eternal life and the power of resurrection" (CCC 1524).

This is why almost every single appearance of the resurrected Christ in Scripture happens in the context of a meal, and when the day is named, on a Sunday. These appearances—on the road to Emmaus, in the Upper Room, on the beach—all have Eucharistic overtones. Jesus breaks bread with his Apostles and feeds his Apostles, and as he does, he helps us understand that the Resurrection renders his body into something that is now distributable, communicable, and edible. His body has been glorified and his humanity deified, and as it enters into us, it creates the capacity within us to be glorified and deified too, to be resurrected on the last day.

Again, "I am the living bread which came down from heaven; if any one eats of this bread, he will live for ever . . . he who eats my flesh and drinks my blood has eternal life, and I will raise him up at the last day" (John 6:51, 54).

What will happen, though, after that? What comes after "the last day"?

CHAPTER 7

THE RENOVATION
OF THE UNIVERSE

Not long ago, I had a conversation with someone who isn't Catholic but was sincerely trying to understand what we Catholics believe about the Eucharist. He couldn't, though. No matter what I said, he couldn't wrap his head around the idea that a mortal man could put his hands over bread and wine, repeat some words spoken by Jesus two millennia ago, and change that bread and wine into the Body and Blood of Jesus Christ.

I did my best to help him understand that these men weren't acting on their own power. By virtue of their ordination, they were empowered to act *in persona Christi*—in the person of Christ. They had received that power from their bishop, who received it from another bishop, who received it from another and another and another. This line of succession—one bishop passing on to another this power to act *in persona Christi*—went all the way back to the Apostles, who in turn had received it from Jesus himself.

The man still wasn't buying it. And part of me couldn't blame him.

As Catholics, we are so used to these ideas—transubstantiation, ordination, consecration, apostolic succession—that we don't always see how truly fantastic they are. I mean, we actually believe bread becomes Body—the Body of Christ, the Body of God made man. We also believe that this Body imparts God's own life to us—that it makes our bodies into living temples of the living God.

Apart from faith, that stretches the mind to the point of incredulity. There's no way it can be true. Unless it is.

The fact is, the Eucharist is far more unbelievable than we let ourselves believe. It's important to recognize that. We can't let ourselves take this truth for granted. We need to see it as the radical act of grace it is. When we do that, we can better appreciate the true glory of what takes place on the altar at every single Mass. More importantly, we can start to appreciate the greater glory that transubstantiation makes possible—the resurrection of our bodies—and the even greater glory to which transubstantiation points—the glory of what's to come.

The First Parousia

Before we talk about the glory to come, though, let's review what we believe about the glory that is: the Eucharist.

When we receive the Eucharist, we receive Jesus Christ, Body and Blood, Soul and Divinity. This is what every Catholic child learns before he or she receives First Holy Communion, and this is the ancient belief of the Church, taught to us by Jesus himself: "My flesh is food indeed, and my blood is drink indeed" (John 6:55). "This is my body . . . This is my blood" (Matt 26:26–28).

In the Eucharist, Jesus Christ is really and truly present. His presence is as real as it was when he walked the streets of Jerusalem and as real as it will be when he returns at the end of days. It is a true *parousia*, a true coming. And it changes us.

At every Mass, in every Holy Communion, Jesus gives his divine life to us. As we've talked about already, the Church calls this life sanctifying grace. It's the life that God breathed into Adam at the dawn of creation and that Adam and Eve both possessed until they made the mistake of listening to the serpent. Sanctifying grace is what they lost, and it's what Jesus restores to us in Baptism.

The Eucharist is God continuing to nourish us with that gift. He feeds us with himself to give our souls what they need for our journey through this world. When we receive the Eucharist frequently, worthily, and reverently, we are healed. We are comforted. We are strengthened. We are empowered to live the life God calls us to live, make the sacrifices he calls us to make, and be the people he calls us to be. The Eucharist, in short, helps us to become holy. It helps us to become saints.

That doesn't happen, though, simply because we are receiving the Body and Blood, Soul and Divinity, of Jesus Christ. In the Eucharist, we are receiving even more.

To say this—that when we receive the Eucharist, we receive more than Jesus Christ, King of Kings and Lord of Lords—sounds impossible. How can we receive *anything* more?

But we do. Because wherever the Son is, the Father and Holy Spirit are present too.

So, when you receive Jesus, the entirety of the Holy Trinity is right there, on your tongue. And wherever you have the Holy Trinity, you also have the Blessed Virgin Mary, the angels, and all the saints. And, wherever they are, you also have the New Creation, the Paschal Mystery, and every single doctrine that the Church proclaims.

We don't just swallow the Eucharist in Holy Communion. We swallow the Creed. We swallow the story of Revelation, the Gospel, the Deposit of Faith, every truth we profess, and every moment in salvation history. All that is on our tongue in Holy Communion. All that is in the tabernacle of every Catholic Church in every city around the world.

There is more glory in one consecrated host than the mind can even begin to properly appreciate. And that glory feeds our bodies and souls, preparing them not just for the journey through this life but also for what comes at journey's end.

Mysteriously, miraculously, when a priest, a mortal man, puts his hands over bread and wine, that bread and wine become Body and Blood. Then, when we receive that Body and Blood, when we take it into our bodies, it incorporates us into the Body of Christ, making it possible for us to be resurrected, body and soul, in Christ.

Transubstantiation, in effect, is a kind of nuclear fusion. It sets into motion a process that will create something entirely new: a new us.

Responding to the question, "How is it possible for the dead to rise again, in their own bodies?" the Catechism states that the answer "exceeds our imagination and understanding; it is accessible only to faith" (CCC 1000). Then, it points to the Eucharist, explaining:

> Our participation in the Eucharist already gives us a foretaste of Christ's transfiguration of our bodies: "Just as bread that comes from the earth, after God's blessing has been invoked upon it, is no longer ordinary bread, but Eucharist, formed of two things, the one earthly and the other heavenly: so too our bodies, which partake of the Eucharist, are no longer corruptible, but possess the hope of resurrection."[1] (CCC 1000)

Remember, this is what Jesus told us when he preached to the crowds in John 6: "He who eats my flesh and drinks my blood has eternal life, and I will raise him up at the last day" (6:54).

When we consume the Eucharist, we consume the means to our own resurrection. Holy Communion after Holy Communion, the Body of Christ empowers our bodies, making them into bodies that can rise again, bodies that can live forever, bodies that can be glorified like Christ's own body.

And if a mortal man, acting *in persona Christi* and saying the words of consecration, can help effect that kind of transformation, imagine what kind of change Jesus Christ as the eternal high priest can effect at the end of days. Imagine what kind of glory will shine forth when the ultimate reality

---

[1]   St. Irenaeus, *Adv. Haeres.* 4, 18, 4–5: PG 7/1, 1028–1029.

to which the Eucharist points manifests itself at the Final Judgment.

The New Heavens and New Earth

In Isaiah 11 and later in the Book of Revelation, both Isaiah and St. John refer to the earth as having "four corners" (Isa 11:12; Rev 7:1). This was a common way of talking about the world, and it's not because they were members of the Flat Earth Society. It's because they saw the earth as an altar, a very specific altar: the altar God instructed Moses to build in Exodus. That altar had four corners, with a horn on each corner, and was where the Levitical priests offered sacrifices of atonement to the Lord (Exod 27:2).

What is the connection between the two, between the world as envisioned by Isaiah and John and the altar of the Old Testament?

I think it will be made plain in the last days. During the time of the eschaton, we're told that the Church, the Body of Christ, will undergo great trials, trials analogous in many ways to the trials that Jesus's physical body underwent two thousand years ago. The Church will be beaten, bloodied, and mocked. Her members will suffer rejection, persecution, and martyrdom. Her priests will be imprisoned, tortured, and executed. Then, finally, Jesus will come again.

When he does, I believe he will say to all the priests being martyred, "Well done, good and faithful servants. You've done what you were asked to do. Now, step aside. It's my turn."

Then, he will put his hands over the altar of the earth and say, "This is my Body." But this time it won't be bread and wine transubstantiated. It will be the heavens and the earth. It will be all the dust and all the bones of all the saints, in all the ages, which will be transubstantiated into the glorified Body of Christ.

Never forget: The Church is not a body metaphorically. The Church is a body metaphysically. And we're not going to cease being members of that Body when we get our resurrected bodies. We are going to get a body like Jesus has a body. We are going to get resurrected, glorified bodies. But we're also going to enter into an even deeper communion with the Body of Christ. We are going to be members of Christ's body in a more real and more true way than my arms and legs are members of my body right now.

This is what St. Paul is getting at in 1 Corinthians 15— that the climax of all the Masses ever celebrated will be the eschaton, the *parousia*, the real presence of the Lord of Lords, in his body, and we will be part of that:

> We shall not all sleep, but we shall all be changed, in a moment, in the twinkling of an eye, at the last trumpet. For the trumpet will sound, and the dead will be raised imperishable, and we shall be changed. For this perishable nature must put on the imperishable, and this mortal nature must put on immortality. When the perishable puts on the imperishable, and the mortal puts on immortality, then shall come to pass the saying that is written: "Death is swallowed up in victory." (1 Cor 15:51–54)

At the eschaton, our bodies will be changed from perishable to imperishable. The Body of Christ on earth will also be changed. All the things which mar her beauty in time—the sins and mistakes and foolish behavior of her members—will fall away, and we will see the Church for what she truly is: Mother, Bride, and Body, perfected in glory. The Second Vatican Council's *Lumen Gentium* states:

> The Church, to which we are all called in Christ Jesus, and in which we acquire sanctity through the grace of God, will attain its full perfection only in the glory of heaven, when there will come the time of the restoration of all things. At that time the human race as well as the entire world, which is intimately related to man and attains to its end through him, will be perfectly reestablished in Christ.[2]

Importantly, as the passage quoted above tells us, it's not just our bodies and the Church that will be transformed at the end of time: It's the entire world . . . and more. As the Catechism says, "the universe itself will be renewed" (CCC 1042). This "mysterious renewal" (CCC 1043) of all that exists in time and space is what Sacred Scripture refers to when it speaks of a "new heavens and a new earth" (2 Pet 3:13), and a "heavenly Jerusalem," where the kingdom of God comes in its fullness and the God of all makes "his dwelling among men" (CCC 1044).

In this new, transformed universe, "he will wipe away

---

[2] Second Vatican Council, *Lumen Gentium* (1964), §48.

every tear" (Rev 21:4), all pain, all sorrow, all mourning will cease, and God will share himself "in an inexhaustible way" with his children. This is what the Church calls "the Beatific Vision," and it will offer to all those saved "the ever-flowing well-spring of happiness, peace, and mutual communion" (CCC 1045).

Quoting St. Paul's Letter to the Romans, the Catechism concludes:

> For the cosmos, Revelation affirms the profound common destiny of the material world and man: For the creation waits with eager longing for the revealing of the sons of God . . . in hope because the creation itself will be set free from its bondage to decay. . . . We know that the whole creation has been groaning in travail together until now; and not only the creation, but we ourselves, who have the first fruits of the Spirit, groan inwardly as we wait for adoption as sons, the redemption of our bodies. The visible universe, then, is itself destined to be transformed, "so that the world itself, restored to its original state, facing no further obstacles, should be at the service of the just," sharing their glorification in the risen Jesus Christ. (CCC 1046–47)

The Second Parousia

Before we talk more about the creation to come, let's back up for a moment to what will come before that for each of us: death.

At the moment of death, the soul leaves its body. While the body begins the long, slow process of decay, the soul immediately experiences the first judgment, usually referred to as our "particular judgment" (CCC 1022). In the particular judgment, we discover the consequences of the choices we made for or against Christ in our lifetime. If, during our earthly life, we accepted the graces of salvation offered to us, we learn that our eternal fate is heaven. Our eternal fate is God. If, however, during our earthly life, we rejected the graces of salvation, our eternal fate is hell. Our eternal fate is not God.

At this point, there are no do-overs. The time for choosing between God and not God ends when we leave this life. The judgment rendered against us is final. And that judgment is just.

Jesus Christ, the divine judge, sees all and knows all. He knows every drop of grace that was offered to us in every moment of our lives. He knows every circumstance that might have inhibited us from freely choosing grace. And he knows the deepest and truest desires of our heart. If the judgment rendered against us at the end of our days is hell, it's because hell is what we chose. Hell is what we desire.

Those who choose hell go there immediately. They don't pass Go. They don't collect $200. They forever leave the presence of God.

Those who said yes to the graces of salvation, those who choose God, go one of two places. Either they immediately enter the company of the blessed in heaven or they pass through a process of purification—purgatory—which will make it possible for them to eventually and fully enter into the joys of heaven.

Again, our eternal fate is decided at the moment of our death, in our particular judgment. But there is another judgment still to come: the Last Judgment.

We are told that at the end of days "all the dead will rise," and that "the hour is coming when all who are in the tombs will hear his voice and come forth, those who have done good, to the resurrection of life, and those who have done evil, to the resurrection of judgment" (CCC 998; John 5:29).

During this Final Judgment, everything you and I have ever done—good and bad—will be made known before all of humanity. Every secret sin, every secret good deed, will be secret no more. Everyone will see. Everyone will know.

Then, after all the judgments have been rendered, the blessed and the damned alike will get their bodies back. For the damned, those bodies will increase their sorrow and pain. For the blessed, those bodies will increase their joy, enabling them to enter more fully into the glories of heaven.

And now, it's time to talk about those bodies.

CHAPTER 8

THE BODY GLORIFIED

If you remember what we talked about in Chapter 2, you'll recall that God didn't design the human body and soul to be separated. He created the human person as a union of body and soul, and, had Adam never sinned, that unity would have remained intact. The separation that occurs at death is a consequence of original sin.

Jesus, by dying and rising again, opened up the path to reunification. Just as his body and soul were joined once more when he was resurrected, transformed, and glorified, so too will all the bodies and souls of all the just be reunited when we are resurrected, transformed, and glorified. The body that the soul rejoins will be your body—the same body reading these words right now—but it will also be different.

How this is possible—technically possible—is a mystery. Saints and theologians have speculated on it for the past two thousand years. How will the body to come be connected to the body that is? What will it look like? What will it do? At what age will it be resurrected? Will babies who die get the bodies of resurrected babies or will their resurrected bodies be all grown up?

Humans have so many questions about the resurrection . . . but unfortunately, God has given us very few answers.

According to the Catechism, when it comes to the resurrection of our bodies, we know exactly five things: 1) "God . . . will definitively grant incorruptible life to our bodies by reuniting them with our souls, through the power of Jesus' Resurrection"; 2) "All the dead will rise"; 3) "All of them will rise again with their own bodies which they now bear"; 4) Our resurrection is connected with the Eucharist; and 5) This resurrection will happen on "the last day" (CCC 997–1001).

That's it. That's all we can definitively say about what lies behind the veil. Everything else "exceeds our imagination and understanding; it is accessible only to faith" (CCC 1000).

Of course, however, that hasn't stopped saints and theologians from saying a bit more through the centuries.

Your Body . . . Only Different

Most of the great Catholic minds who have wrestled with the questions surrounding the resurrection of our bodies have gone back to St. Paul's words in 1 Corinthians 15, which is the fullest treatment on the subject Sacred Scripture gives us. There Paul explains that the relationship between our earthly and heavenly bodies is like that of a seed to the wheat that grows from the seed: "And what you sow is not the body which is to be, but a bare kernel, perhaps of wheat or of some other grain" (1 Cor 15:37).

This idea of continuity between seed and grain inspired a host of other metaphors to explain how exactly God could bring back together bodies that had long since turned to dust. Rebuilt temples, reforged pots, and rebuilt ships were among the favorites. So was the mythical phoenix, rising from the ashes. But no matter how people tried to explain the resurrection, it all came down to a matter of faith and a question of trust. As Tertullian, writing in second century Carthage, insisted, "God is quite able to remake what he once made."[1]

A thousand years later, St. Thomas Aquinas drew upon the work of the early Church Fathers to flesh out the Church's most detailed reflection upon what these resurrected bodies of ours will be like. According to Aquinas, all resurrected bodies have three "conditions"—that is, identifiable traits—in common.[2]

The first of these conditions is quality. Here, quality has two aspects. The first pertains to a specific attribute of the resurrected body: namely, sex. According to Aquinas, sex isn't going away in heaven. If your body is male in this life, it will be male in the next. Likewise, if your body is female in this life, it will be female in the next. God created the human person male and female, and that's how it's going to stay.

This may seem like stating the obvious, but to both the Gnostics in Christianity's first centuries and the Cathars (or Albigensians) in Aquinas's day, it wasn't. Both heresies asserted that women couldn't enter heaven until they had

---

[1] Tertullian, *On the Resurrection of the Flesh*, 11.
[2] For Aquinas's full treatment of the resurrected body, see *Summa Theologiae* III, supp., qq. 75–85.

been miraculously transformed into men. By stressing that "quality," in part, refers to the nature of the thing, Aquinas was helping counter that error.

There is another aspect to "quality," though, and it has to do with the condition or shape the resurrected body will be in. Aquinas posited that no matter what age we die—at ninety-nine years old or nine minutes old—our resurrected bodies will all be resurrected at what he calls "the most perfect stage of nature."[3] That is to say, our bodies will be resurrected in the peak of their physical strength, health, and attractiveness.

The second condition common to all resurrected bodies that Aquinas named is identity, meaning your body will still be your body and you will still be you. The same soul you have now will once more be united to the same body (albeit resurrected and glorified) that you have now. This, however, doesn't mean you will look exactly like you look now (or even how you looked at your "prime age"). Remember, after Jesus's Resurrection, his closest friends and family didn't always recognize him. Sometimes they did. But sometimes they didn't. Sometimes he looked like himself. Sometimes he didn't.

Aquinas says the same will hold true for us. Fortunately, he adds, because it will be heaven, we won't experience the difficulties the Apostles did when it comes to recognizing our friends and loved ones. God will make sure that we recognize Grandma Jane and Uncle Joe on sight, no matter how different their resurrected bodies might look from how we remember them.

---

[3] Aquinas, *Summa Theologiae* III, supp., q. 81, a. 1.

That brings us to the third condition of our bodies to come: integrity. No matter what happens to your body in this life, in the next life it will be whole. People who lost limbs on earth will have those limbs back in heaven. People who couldn't see or hear while they were alive on earth will see and hear in heaven. And people whose bodies were utterly destroyed in death, whose bodies were ravaged by fire, whose bones were crushed to dust, or whose whole physical selves were obliterated by a nuclear blast—all those people will have their bodies restored to them in their entirety in heaven. This is essentially what Tertullian meant when he wrote, "Any loss sustained by our bodies is an accident to them, but their entirety is their natural property. . . . To nature, not to injury are we restored."[4]

Your Body . . . Only Better

All resurrected bodies—the bodies of the good and the bodies of the wicked, will be of the same nature that they were in life. They will still be identifiably our body, and they will be whole, complete, and intact. The bodies of the blessed, however, that are resurrected to eternal life with God, will have four additional conditions.

The first of these conditions is impassibility. Drawing upon St. Paul's words about the resurrected body, "What is sown is perishable, what is raised is imperishable" (1 Cor 15:42), Aquinas interprets this to mean that the resurrected bodies of the blessed cannot grow sick, cannot feel pain,

---

[4] Tertullian, *On the Resurrection of the Flesh*, 57.

cannot age, and cannot die. They will be incorruptible, utterly exempt from the effects of illness, injury, or time. They also won't be subject to bodily passions like lust or hunger, and will have no need to eat (although they can eat) or engage in sexual intercourse.

The second condition of those resurrected to eternal life that Aquinas names is subtlety. This means that our bodies—while real, concrete, and present in space and time—will also possess a lightness that makes them almost ethereal. That doesn't mean they will be able to walk through walls; that is a miracle. But, the heaviness of them that we experience in this life will be absent. We also will possess the power to fully communicate ourselves—our thoughts, feelings, the whole essence of who we are—to others. All the things in this life that make it difficult for us to understand others or share ourselves with others will disappear in the next.

The third condition listed by Aquinas is agility. So, the body that is "sown in weakness . . . is raised in power" (1 Cor 15:43). By agility, Aquinas doesn't just mean our resurrected bodies will be more coordinated than they are on earth. He means they will be perfectly coordinated, in a way that the movements of the greatest athletes and the greatest ballet dancers can only hint at. Basically, our bodies will do whatever we want them to do, and they will do it perfectly: they will dunk basketballs, do pirouettes, leap tall buildings, and fly through the air. Every desire we have in this life—to move gracefully or swiftly, to soar through the sky or effortlessly float above it all—we have because that's what our bodies were, in a sense, made to do. In heaven, we'll be able to do it all with ease.

Agility also means we'll be able to immediately realize

other desires—to be where we want to be immediately, to see who we want to see immediately, to do what we want to do immediately. If you want to stand in a green meadow in heaven, all you will have to do is think that thought, and you'll be there. If you want to see your great-great-great grandpa in heaven, you will . . . instantaneously, as soon as you want to see him. Essentially, your body will travel at the speed of your thoughts. It will be completely subject to your mind, not to the earthly laws of space and time.

None of these movements of the glorified body, however, will be dictated by our whims. Every movement we make will be inspired by divine wisdom and ordered to knowing and loving God better, by both showing forth more clearly and perceiving more fully the glory of his creation and the beauty of all his saints.

The final quality Aquinas says the glorified bodies of the blessed will possess is clarity. On one level, this means our bodies will be brilliant—literally. "And those who are wise shall shine like the brightness of the firmament; and those who turn many to righteousness, like the stars for ever and ever," says the Book of Daniel (12:3). This is what all those pictures of saints with halos are trying to get at. Those images only convey a fraction of the truth, though, a truth that tells us that all the blessed will be like Jesus at the Transfiguration, when his face "shone like the sun," and his "garments became white as light" (Matt 17:2). That light is holiness, and in heaven everyone will possess it. Holiness will radiate from us. We will be lit from within by the fire of God's love, and that love will make us, quite literally, radiantly beautiful.

Clarity means more than just brilliance, though. Here,

right now, "the body expresses the person."[5] Our bodies make visible the invisible truths about us. But they don't do it perfectly. Someone can't look at us and automatically know everything about us—what we love, what we know, how we've suffered, or what we're capable of doing. Despite the witness of our bodies, much about who we are remains obscured, even to the people who know us best. I know my wife Kimberly better than anyone but God. I know her soul better than anyone but God. But for all I know here on earth, there's still more I don't know.

In heaven, with our resurrected bodies, that will change. I will truly know Kimberly then, and Kimberly will truly know me. Everyone will. Everyone will know each other perfectly at a glance. Illuminated by the light of God, our bodies will perfectly express who we are. Every wound and every scar that has been accepted for the love of God and offered back to him will shine with glory. Again, our souls will literally shine, animating our entire being, so that there is no truth about us that isn't made manifest in our bodies.

That is what our bodies, by grace, are destined to be in the next life. The bodies that frustrate us with their weakness, cripple us with illness and injury, and slow us down with age will become matter infused and suffused with glory. They will be capable of feats that even the most powerful superheroes would never attempt in comic books. And they will image us and image Christ perfectly, beautifully, effortlessly, forever, in the presence of God.

What will these bodies do, though, once they enter into the presence of God in some transformed universe?

[5] John Paul II, *Man and Woman He Created Them*, 183.

CHAPTER 9

✠

YOUR BODY AT
HOME AT LAST

All too often, when people think about the Beatific Vision, they picture themselves sitting and staring at the Father, gazing into his eyes for a billion years. They think of heaven almost like it's some kind of everlasting staring contest, with us looking at God and God looking at us and everyone trying not to blink. Others think of it more like looking at a computer screen, with humanity sitting before the Trinity and downloading all the knowledge God possesses and wants to give us.

Both sound interesting enough at first, but after a billion years . . . definitely less so. After all, who wants to stare at anything for a billion years? Even if who we're staring at is God. Eventually, it seems like it's bound to get boring.

Fortunately, God's not giving us resurrected and glorified bodies to just stare at him for all eternity. God is a Father, and when a father sits with his children, his attitude isn't "All eyes on me." A father doesn't want his children doing nothing but sitting and staring at him! A father wants to talk with his children, tell them stories, and help them understand their own story better. A father wants to fill his children with life and help them to live life to the fullest. A father also wants to see his children sharing their stories with each other, learning from each other, and loving each other.

Something like that, I think, is what we're going to experience in heaven when we look into the Father's eyes.

The Greatest Symphony Ever Played

In heaven, if the Father is truly a father, I believe we're going to gaze into his eyes and see our story—the whole story, from the first second we were conceived to the last breath we breathed and even beyond that, to all the ways our life continued to affect the world after our death.

Try as we might, we can't see that whole story here. We're finite creatures, limited by space and time. When we look at our lives, we only see them from one perspective— our perspective. We also only see them in part—the parts that were and are, past and present—not the parts to come. And even the past and present we see imperfectly, with our emotions, faulty memories, and limited perspective clouding our vision.

Our human brains can only hold so much here on earth. God, though, is infinite. He isn't limited by space or time. Also, the mind of God is omniscient. He sees all—every moment and every story—and he knows all—how every moment and every story is connected to every other moment and every other story. In heaven, that is what God will impart to us.

When we finally enter into the Beatific Vision, we will understand why our days unfolded as they did, why we carried the crosses we did, and why we experienced the blessings we did. We also will see why we made the choices we did, what graces God gave us, and what spiritual battles took place around us while we ate and slept and worked and prayed.

In heaven, our lives—the everlasting whole of them—will make sense to us. We won't question why something unfolded as it did or feel like we got short-changed or wonder how God could have asked us to endure certain crosses. We will know and see it all, and we will think it perfect, from first to last, recognizing how there wasn't a moment lost or wasted and how even the tragedies of our life contribute to the joy and beauty of heaven.

In a sense, it's like all of our lives and all of time form a symphony that no human could write and no master musician could perform. And when we hear that symphony in heaven, we will understand how all the dark experiences, all the tragedies, all the minor chords and dissonant sounds contributed something important, making the whole greater and more beautiful than the sum of its parts.

And that's God's handiwork. God, in his wisdom, brings an overarching unity and beauty out of all the dissonance. By his power, even the tragic elements of our story will become comic or joyful. Even sin, even true evil, won't mar but will show forth the beauty of the music God is composing in his providence. The crucifixion, the greatest evil ever perpetrated by mankind on Good Friday, became the wellspring for the greatest good imaginable: the Resurrection of Jesus Christ and the salvation of mankind. In the same way, all the sorrows and tragedies of our lives will somehow become a wellspring of glory.

But it's not just our story making up that symphony. It's not just our life that we're going to see and understand in the Father's eyes. It's our mother's and our father's story, our spouse's and our best friend's. It's the story of the guy who worked in the cubicle next to us when we were twenty-four years old and the story of the neighbor across the street with whom we never spoke and the story of the anchorman on the evening news whom we watched when we were just kids.

The Greatest Story Ever Told

The best dinner party or family gathering you've ever attended, where everyone is feasting and talking and laughing and sharing stories, has nothing on the feasting and talking and laughing and sharing stories that will take place in heaven. Our greatest experiences of love, connection, and friendship here on earth offer us only the tiniest foretaste of the love, connection, and friendship we will experience in heaven, where every story will be shared and every story will be endlessly fascinating. Every story will be beautiful and interesting and compelling and engaging. Every story will make us laugh and weep for the joy of it all. Not one story will be boring. Not one story won't hold our attention. Not one story won't utterly and completely captivate us.

Moreover, as everyone tells their stories, every other

person is going to see how their own stories were connected to that story—how they were blessed or changed or strengthened or challenged in some way because of every single other person's story.

In life, we pass strangers on the street, sit next to them on subways, and watch them on screens in our living rooms, all the while thinking these people have nothing to do with us. We see their stories as their stories and our story as our story and can't imagine how they could possibly be connected.

When we see others' stories through the Father's eyes, though, we will see them for what they truly are: one story, the same story, our story. The Catechism explains, "*For man, this consummation will be the final realization of the unity of the human race, which God willed from creation and of which the pilgrim Church has been 'in the nature of sacrament'*" (CCC 1045).

The Beatific Vision is going to light up the connections between your story and my story and the story of every other person on this planet—every person who is, was, and ever shall be.

God loves stories. The very best storytellers in all of human history are made in his image. And their power to tell a story is just a pale reflection of his power to tell a story. God wrote the story of the universe. He wrote the story of our salvation. He wrote my story and your story and the story of every man, woman, and child who has ever walked this earth. He orchestrates every detail of every life, working with and through our free will, in order to lead us to him. That's the goal. Not earthly power, wealth, comfort, or happiness. But everlasting life and joy in heaven with him.

Again, though, the stories God writes, the lives he

scripts, aren't separate. They are one. They are all part of one great story that nobody but he can see. He sees it all—how every story is connected to every other story and how every story fits into the one great story. All our lives are like puzzle pieces that fit together to form the greatest story ever told. Every once in a while, in life, we get the smallest glimpses of that. We run into a random person on a plane or in a restaurant on the other side of the world and discover that we grew up in the same town or worked for the same person or share a mutual friend. And when we make that discovery, there is a little flash of joy—that recognition of "Oh, you too! You know something of my story! You share some part of my story!"

The Greatest Dance Ever Danced

That, writ large and for days without end, is what we'll experience in heaven. Here, we see just a sliver of the ties binding us to others and just a sliver of the story God is writing. But in heaven, we will see it all. We will see how we are all part of one story and one family and one body, and that the most seemingly random and disjointed episodes in our life weren't random at all. They were part of this perfect story, where nobody is unimportant to the plot. C. S. Lewis calls this the "Great Dance":

> In the plan of the Great Dance plans without number interlock, and each movement becomes in its season the breaking into flower of the whole design to which all else has been directed. Thus each is

equally at the center, and none are there by being equals, but some by giving place and some by receiving it, the small things by their smallness and the great by their greatness, and all the patterns linked and looped together by the unions of kneeling with a sceptered love.[1]

In other words, in heaven we're going to see how the choices we made affected others, shaped others, and blessed others in a way that is beyond coincidence, beyond happenstance or chance. We also are going to see how others affected, shaped, and blessed us, helping us along to the Father in ways we never guessed or imagined or could even began to fathom in this life.

Right now, someone in this world is praying for you. Someone else is putting a plan into motion that will help you in some way ten, twenty, or thirty years down the road. Another person is making a good choice today that will spare you suffering tomorrow. When you, in your resurrected body, look into the Father's eyes, you will see that. You will see the people who blessed you. And you will see the people you blessed—the random strangers for whom someone on social media asked you to pray, the great-great-great grandchildren who exist because you said yes to one more baby, the loving wife and mother who didn't die in a fiery wreck on the highway because you didn't violate the speed limit.

All those choices matter. Every one of them. And in heaven, you will see the fruit of them. You'll see the people who blessed you and whom you blessed. You'll talk with

---

[1] C. S. Lewis, *Perelandra* (New York: Macmillan, 1944), 217.

them and laugh with them and experience a connection of love and grace like nothing you've ever experienced here on earth. The deepest connection you have ever felt with anyone in this life is nothing more than a shadow of the connection you will experience with every single person in heaven.

The Body's Role

Maybe it will take at least a billion years to discover all those connections—to tell our stories and hear everyone else's stories. Maybe it will take at least a billion more to digest them and another billion to understand them. But it doesn't matter. Because, after all that, after every story has been told and retold, we'll still want to keep hearing them over and over, loving every retelling and discovering something new each time.

Your favorite movie that you've watched again and again, your favorite book that you've read over and over, your favorite album that you could listen to on repeat for days—all those things can't compare to how many times you will want to hear the story of the world's salvation. No one will ever grow bored of it. No one will ever grow tired of it. No one will ever feel like they've learned all they can learn or heard all they can hear.

And through it all, the very body that is reading these words, on this page, right now, will be experiencing that joy. It will be part of it. Reunited to your soul at last, glorified and filled with *zoe*, your body won't just be hearing stories, it will be telling *your* story. And it will be telling your story not just with words, but with the life that has been written on it.

The scars from your C-section, the arm you broke playing football with your son, the hands calloused from working long hours in the service of others, the laugh lines earned because you smiled so often at so many—all those things will be telling the story of you in heaven, much like they do on earth, but more perfectly, powerfully, and beautifully. Those marks and scars that seemed like imperfections in life will shine with glory in heaven, making the love of God manifest in a way that is beyond words.

So too will everyone else's marks and scars.

In heaven, you will see the wounds of Christ's Passion and execution on him with your own eyes, and you will rejoice that those wounds haven't been wiped away. You also will see martyrs, whose bodies still bear the marks of their deaths but bear them in a way so beautiful it takes your breath away. Just as my wife Kimberly's body is more beautiful to me because of what pregnancy, childbirth, and motherhood have done to it, the bodies of the saints will be more beautiful for the lives on earth that were lived in them. The agility, subtlety, and impassability of every single resurrected body that surrounds you in heaven will be all the greater for the serving and sacrificing, loving and suffering those bodies did on earth.

Moreover, every person's body will radiate the truth of the person and the truth of their story and the truth of the Greatest Story ever told. After all, those bodies were part of the story. Every bit as much as the souls that animate them. The story of us and the story of the world's salvation is written, in some way, on each and every one of our bodies. And the mere thought that anyone would burn part of that story, that someone would willfully reduce to ash such a crucial element of that holy sacred tale, would fill your heavenly self with horror.

When you know this, when you see this, you can't help but see your body differently. You can't help but see death differently. And you can't help but see the dead body differently. The witness of history attests to this.

CHAPTER 10

THE WITNESS
OF HISTORY

Everyone, at some point or another, is afraid of the dark
. . . and not just children. Walking into a dark room—a
room we don't know, a room that's not familiar—is enough
to make even grown men nervous. We just aren't sure what
we'll find there. Little children imagine monsters. Adults
more realistically imagine stubbing our toes.

Either way, darkness inspires fear. It always has. And
for thousands upon thousands of years, what came after
this life was shrouded in darkness. No one knew what happened to the human person after death. They had theories
and guesses, of course. The religions of the ancient world
are built around those theories and guesses, with Egyptian
pharaohs claiming they would become gods after death,
Israelites speculating about *Sheol*, and the ancient Greeks
devising elaborate myths about the Underworld.

Nevertheless, despite all the comfort people tried to
derive from those myths, death was still a dark room, and

fear remained. Occasionally, you had philosophers such as Socrates who seemed to face death with calm and courage. There also were the Stoics, whose adherents claimed they could look death in the face and not blink. But they were the exception. The vast majority of people in the ancient world, for all their familiarity with death, for all the death that surrounded them, saw death and shrank from it.

But then Jesus came. And that changed everything.

Death and the Underworld

Christianity was first preached in a world where the Greco-Roman understanding of death and the afterlife shaped much of the Western world. Across the Roman Empire, most people professed their faith in the various pagan gods, including Pluto (or Hades), who they believed ruled the Underworld. At the Underworld's entrance, the ferryman Charon moved spirits across the River Styx from the land of the living to the land of the dead. Once they made it to the other side, all the dead faced judgment, with the good going to Elysium, the bad being thrown into the pit of Tartarus, and the mediocre rest (the majority of humanity) aimlessly drifting about in the City of Pluto (or what the Greeks called the Asphodel Meadows). Some Romans also believed those who'd been judged worthy could choose to be reincarnated.

This vision of the afterlife offered some consolation to those who actually believed it, but not enough. Most Romans, like most of humanity, still feared what awaited them in the dark room of death. And that fear manifested itself in how they treated their dead.

The pagan Romans thought that if dead bodies weren't treated a certain way and certain conditions weren't met, the person's soul would be denied admittance to the Underworld. Rather than receiving its eternal reward, the soul would instead endure an almost purgatory-like existence, waiting perpetually on the wrong side of the River Styx. The Romans also believed that if they failed to provide their departed loved ones with a proper burial, those waiting ghosts would return to haunt them.

For the rich, preventing this two-headed fate was a simple matter. They paid for elaborate funerals and lengthy funeral processions, which included professional mourners and friends wearing masks designed to look like the ancestors of the deceased. They also made sure to place a coin on or in the dead person's mouth so that the soul could pay Charon to ferry them across the River Styx.

After the funeral procession concluded, a eulogy was often given. Next, the body was placed on a pyre and burned. The remaining ashes and bones were then placed in an urn, which was interred in some kind of sepulcher—usually highly decorated, with monuments to the deceased and even lifelike pictures of them. Those sepulchers were located outside the city gates, as the Romans liked to keep their dead far from them, at a "safe" distance. They did visit the sepulcher on various days throughout the year, though, believing that by making periodic offerings to their dearly departed, what remained of the person—their "shade"—would temporarily remember who they once were and earn a brief reprieve from aimlessly wandering about the Underworld.

For the poor, funerals were less impressive, with the funerary societies they frequently joined (for a small fee) providing shorter processions (just a musician or two), no eulogy, and interment of the ashes in a humbler resting site—often catacombs carved into clay and rock outside the city.

The poorest of the poor didn't even have that. Those with no family or friends to fear a haunting and no money to join a funerary society were simply thrown into large pits or dumped into sewers.

In the late third and fourth centuries, many of these practices among the pagan Romans began to change, with inhumation (burial) gradually replacing cremation. Although some Romans had buried their dead in previous centuries, inhumation was considered a foreign (more specifically, Jewish) practice. The growing presence of Christians in their midst, however, along with other social shifts, changed that.

Delivered from Fear

For the Christians, like the Romans, how they treated the dead was bound up with what they believed about life after death. But unlike their pagan counterparts, the Christians didn't fear death. They welcomed it. Writing in the early fourth century, St. Athanasius remarked: "Everyone is by nature afraid of death and of bodily dissolution; the marvel of marvels, is that he who is enfolded in the faith of the cross despises this natural fear and for the sake of the cross is no longer cowardly in the face of it."[1]

---

[1] Athanasius, *On the Incarnation*, 58.

When Jesus Christ rose from the dead, he didn't switch a bright overhead light on in heaven, completely destroying the darkness that shrouded what awaits us after death. He gave us more of a night-light, making some things clear while leaving other things a mystery. But to Athanasius and other early Christians, that didn't matter. The night-light was sufficient because Jesus was there. Much like the presence of a mother or father can completely chase away a child's fears of the dark, Jesus's presence chased away the early Christians' fear of death. They knew he would be there to greet them, and that was enough. Athanasius explains:

> Before the divine sojourn of the Savior, even the holiest of men were afraid of death, and mourned the dead as those who perish. But now that the Savior has raised His body, death is no longer terrible, but all those who believe in Christ tread it underfoot as nothing, and prefer to die rather than to deny their faith in Christ, knowing full well that when they die they do not perish, but live indeed and become incorruptible through the resurrection . . . Even children hasten to die, and not men only, but women train themselves by bodily discipline to meet it. So weak has death become that even women, who used to be taken in by it, mock at it now as a dead thing robbed of all its strength.[2]

To those Christian men, women, and children who "hasten[ed] to die," death wasn't the ultimate evil or the great

---

[2] Athanasius, *On the Incarnation,* 57.

unknown. It was the doorway to spending eternity with their beloved: Jesus Christ. We see this conviction in the firsthand accounts of martyrs, such as Sts. Perpetua and Felicity, who faced death in Carthage's arena in AD 203.

Both women were young wives and mothers: Felicity was pregnant at the time of their arrest, and Perpetua was still nursing her infant son. As the day of their death approached, the women didn't want to run from it. Rather, Felicity prayed she would deliver her child soon so that she could face martyrdom with her fellow prisoners (even the Romans thought it beyond the pale to kill a pregnant women), and Perpetua gave thanks when her son finally weaned.

Felicity's prayers were answered, and on the day of the scheduled execution, she accompanied Perpetua and their fellow Christians into the arena, "joyous and of brilliant countenances." Perpetua sang psalms as she walked, and when the crowds demanded that the Christians be scourged before they faced the beasts, the women "rejoiced that they should have incurred any one of their Lord's passions." Finally, the women, like Jesus, freely gave their lives; they were not taken from them. We're told: "when the swordsman's hand wandered still (for he was a novice), [Perpetua] set it upon her own neck. Perchance so great a woman could not else have been slain . . . had she not herself so willed it."[3]

Tame Deaths

In the centuries that followed, holy men and women faced

---

[3] Tertullian, *The Passion of the Holy Martyrs Perpetua and Felicity*, 6.

death with the same eagerness that Perpetua, Felicity, and other earlier martyrs, such as St. Ignatius of Antioch, did. They wanted nothing more than to be in heaven with Christ. As Ignatius, on his way to martyrdom in AD 108, explained:

> No earthly pleasures, no kingdoms of this world can benefit me in any way. I prefer death in Christ Jesus to power over the farthest limits of the earth. He who died in place of us is the one object of my quest. He who rose for our sakes is my one desire.[4]

One thousand years later, that same desire to be with Christ led St. Bernard of Clairvaux to describe the death of a just man not as "terrifying," but as "consoling":

> His death is good, because it ends his miseries; it is better still, because he begins a new life; it is excellent, because it places him in sweet security. From this bed of mourning, whereon he leaves a precious load of virtues, he goes to take possession of the true land of the living, Jesus acknowledges him as His brother and as His friend, for he has died to the world before closing his eyes from its dazzling light. Such is the death of the saints, a death very precious in the sight of God.[5]

---

[4] Ignatius of Antioch, *Letter to the Romans*, 6.
[5] Bernard of Clairvaux, quoted in Charles Kenny, *Half Hours with the Saints and Servants of God* (London: Burns and Oats, 1882), 450.

From the thirteenth century—when St. Rose of Viterbo advised, "Live so as not to fear death. For those who live well in the world, death is not frightening but sweet and precious"—to the nineteenth century, when St. Thérèse of Lisieux wrote: "It is not Death that will come to fetch me, it is the good God"—saint after saint encouraged Christians to welcome death. And many listened.

In Phillipe Ariès's landmark survey of depictions of death in the literature of Western Civilization, he classifies pre-modern deaths as "tame deaths," noting how the protagonists almost universally faced death with calm, peace, and ease. It was death, he explains, that brought people back to their senses, focused their attention, and was welcomed, almost as an old friend.[6]

Ariès likewise notes that even some modern authors sensed this difference between their protagonists and the protagonists of old. In Aleksandr Solzhenitsyn's *The Cancer Ward*, he finds the best summation of how Christians for many long centuries faced death:

> The old folk, who never even made it to town, they were scared, while Yefrem rode horses and fired pistols at thirteen . . . But now . . . he remembered how the old folk used to die back home on the Kama— They didn't puff themselves up or fight against it or brag that they weren't going to die—they took death calmly. They didn't stall, squaring things away, they prepared themselves quietly and in good time . . .

[6] See Phillipe Ariès, *Western Attitudes Toward Death*, trans. Patricia Ranum (Baltimore: Johns Hopkins University Press, 1975), 1–25.

And they departed easily, as if they were just moving into a new house.[7]

Human Bones

Jesus Christ's life, death, and Resurrection radically shaped how his followers faced death. So, not surprisingly, it also shaped how they treated the dead.

After his crucifixion, Jesus, like all Jews of his day, had been buried. With reverence and care, his body was carried from the cross to a tomb. But it didn't stay there. On the third day, Jesus rose from the dead in the transfigured but still selfsame body he had possessed in life. He promised the same fate to those who followed him. So, naturally, Christians weren't going to imitate the pagans and, as Tertullian put it, "burn up their dead with harshest inhumanity."[8] As Tertullian explained elsewhere, those who followed Christ were to "avert a cruel custom with regard to the body since, being human, it does not deserve what is inflicted upon criminals."[9]

And so, from the very first, Christians buried their dead as Christ had been buried, and they did so with no fear of being made "unclean" or "polluted" by contact with the dead body. For the Christians, the dead body wasn't "unclean" (as the Jews saw it), nor did those who handled it fear being haunted by some remnant of the person's soul (as the pagans did).

---

[7]   Aleksandr Solzhenitsyn, *The Cancer Ward*, quoted in Ariès, *Western Attitudes Toward Death,* 13.

[8]   Tertullian, *On the Resurrection of the Flesh*, 1.

[9]   Tertullian, *A Treatise on the Soul*, 51.

Writing in the fourth and fifth centuries, St. Augustine discussed the reverence Christians believed was due to the dead body, noting:

> The bodies of the dead, and especially of the just and faithful are not to be despised or cast aside. The soul has used them as organs and vessels of all good work in a holy manner. . . . Bodies are not ornament or for aid, as something that is applied externally, but pertain to the very nature of the man.[10]

Importantly, Christians understood the injunction to care for and bury the dead as universal; it applied to all bodies—the bodies of the poor, the stranger, the diseased, even the pagan. Accounts about early Christian communities are filled with stories of them seeking out the forgotten poor and burying them with the same care they showed to family members. Tertullian also tells us that in his native Carthage and other cities, the Church's common resources were used to pay for the burying of the dead. There was no throwing the bodies of the poor into a pit or the sewers among the Christians.

Their pagan neighbors took note of that. In his essay "To Bury or Burn?," the Protestant ethicist David W. Jones tells us:

> The last of the non-Christian emperors, Julian the Apostate (ad 332–363), identified "care of the dead" as one of the factors that contributed to the spread of Christianity throughout the Roman world. The

---

[10] Augustine, *On the Care of the Dead*, 5.

church historian Philip Schaff, too, identified Christians' display of "decency to the human body" in showing care for the dead as one of the main reasons for the church's rapid conquest of the ancient world.[11]

In time, burying the dead would become known as one of the seven corporal works of mercy, considered as much an act of charity as feeding the hungry or tending to the sick. Religious associations, such as the Archconfraternity of the Beheaded John the Baptist in Florence and the Archconfraternity of St. Mary of the Oration and Death in Rome, also were formed to offer Christian funerals and burials to those who would otherwise have none.

No bodies, though, not rich nor poor, received as much attention as those of the martyrs.

Holy Bones

In early second century Rome, the two sisters, Sts. Praxedes and Pudentiana, risked their lives venturing into the places where their fellow Christians had been martyred. There, they gathered up the bones, flesh, and even blood left behind. They then brought those remains back to their father's house for burial.

Other Christians followed suit, going to such great lengths to recover the bodies of their martyred friends, that, according to the fourth century Christian historian Eusebius, the Romans had to post guards to prevent Chris-

[11] Jones, "To Bury or Burn?," 337.

tians from stealing the martyrs' remains. Eusebius also tells us that the Romans frequently attempted to add insult to injury by burning the bodies of martyred Christians and scattering their ashes, thinking that in doing so they could dash Christian hopes of resurrection.[12]

It didn't work. As the religious historian Caroline Walker Bynum recounts, Christians explicitly rejected the pagan idea that "delay in burial injures the soul or that persons who die prematurely or violently or receive no burial, will wander the earth as ghosts or demons."[13]

Moreover, early theologians, such as Tertullian, went out of their way to help their fellow Christians understand that the Church didn't oppose cremation because they thought it presented an obstacle to resurrection. Burying bodies was simply a question of respect. God could and would resurrect all bodies, Tertullian assured Christians, no matter what was done to them after death.

Two centuries later, St. Augustine echoed Tertullian when he said, "Earth has not covered many of the bodies of the Christians, but nothing has kept anyone of them from Heaven and Earth."[14]

Those martyrs whose bodies the early Christians could recover, they kept close. Unlike the Romans, who buried their dead outside the city gates, Christians frequently brought the bodies of the martyrs back to their homes and laid them to rest there. Others were buried in catacombs or tombs. Wherever the remains of the martyrs lay, Chris-

---

[12] See Bynum, *The Resurrection of the Body,* 49–50.

[13] Eusebius, *Ecclesiastical History* 5.1.62-63.

[14] Augustine, *On the Care of the Dead,* 4.

tians gathered to venerate the remains.

One of the earliest accounts we have of this comes from the Christian community in Smyrna. In 156, the great saint and bishop Polycarp went to his death. Afterwards, one member of the community recounted in a letter that:

> We took up his bones, which are more valuable than precious stones and finer than refined gold, and laid them in a suitable place, where the Lord will permit us to gather ourselves together, as we are able, in gladness and joy, and to celebrate the birthday of his martyrdom.[15]

Eventually, altars were built over the bodies of these martyrs. Then, with the legalization of Christianity in 313, whole basilicas arose over these graves. Today, many of the Church's holiest sites, including St. Peter's Basilica in Rome, are built over the graves of these martyrs.

Martyrs weren't the only ones buried in churches, though. As more and more churches were built, with the bones of martyrs below their altars or enclosed in tombs nearby, ordinary Christians sought to be buried there as well. While their pagan counterparts wanted their sepulchers adorned with statues, carvings, and paintings paying tribute to their accomplishments in life, the early Christians weren't concerned with tributes. They were fine with anonymity, as long as they were buried in proximity to a saint.

Eventually, this created a problem, as a church can only hold so many bodies. So, with space filling up inside church-

---

[15] *The Martyrdom of Polycarp*, 18.

es, bodies were frequently moved and relocated to charnel houses—sepulchers piled high (and occasionally decorated) with bones. Later, when possible, the land around churches was bought up and used as a burial ground.

Some bones, however, never made it to the grave . . . or charnel house . . . or church.

Blessed Bones

From at least the second century, when Christians gathered around Polycarp's remains, the bones of the saints and martyrs were treated as holy objects, pieces of matter through which grace traveled from God to man and through which God, if he so chose, could work miracles. As such, pieces of bodies and bones were moved from church to church and city to city, not only enabling cities without martyrs to have saints in their churches and under their altars, but also allowing the residents of those cities to venerate the bones and ask for miracles of their own.

Rarely did God disappoint. In 415, when the relics of the first Christian martyr, St. Stephen, arrived in Hippo, the city's bishop, St. Augustine, was so impressed by the number of healings which occurred in conjunction with the relics' arrival that he ordered a book made that recounted every miracle God worked through St. Stephen's relics, both in Hippo and elsewhere.

Unfortunately, such a careful accounting of miracles and even the authenticity of some relics wasn't always possible. The miracles worked by St. Stephen's relics were well documented because priests and guardians traveled with relics.

The Church had entrusted them to care for the bones and ensure that those who venerated them treated them with nothing less than reverence. Not all relics traveled with quite so much ceremony, though. Grave robbery and relic smuggling were, unfortunately, a common practice for many centuries. So too was the selling of relics. The holier the saint, the higher the price.

The Church did not look kindly on that. She frowned upon those who broke into the tombs of the saints to take pieces of their remains (a practice that became increasingly common in the high middle ages). She also tried to prevent the smuggling of whole body parts away from the rest of the corpse (such as when the citizens of Siena traveled to Rome, severed the head from the body of their native daughter, St. Catherine, and brought the head back to their cathedral).

Still, despite the abuse of relics, the Church unfailingly endorsed the veneration of relics and their miracle-working potential.

Writing in the fourth century, Cyril of Jerusalem pointed to the Old Testament, where a body thrown into the grave of the deceased prophet Elisha is brought back to life. That, he argued, was proof that "a power lies in the bodies of the just, even when their souls are not present."[16] St. Jerome also opposed those who argued that bones in general, including the bones of the martyrs, were "unclean" and therefore unworthy of veneration. He explained:

> But we honor the relics of the martyrs that we may
> honor them whose martyrs they are . . . Are the

---

[16] Cyril of Jerusalem, *Catechetical Lectures* 18:16.

relics of Peter and Paul unclean? Is the body of Moses unclean, the body which according to Hebrews was buried by the Lord himself? . . . If it is not permissible to honor the relics of the martyrs, why do we read: "Precious in the eyes of the Lord is the death of his saints?" If their bones pollute what they touch, how did the dead Elias raise a dead man; how did that body which according to Vigilantius is impure give life [to a corpse]?[17]

Whether in the first century or the twenty-first, though, the Catholic veneration of relics was bound up with its understanding of the body and the human person. It was a testament to the union of body and soul and to the power of grace that could make not only a soul holy but a body holy as well.

The power of relics also helped make sense of the resurrection of the body. If grace could make a dead body holy, if it could work a miracle using bones or teeth or hair, then it also could resurrect and transform that body. Moreover, no bones through which miracles flowed could ever simply rot in a grave. They had to be resurrected. They had to one day physically reflect the glory that was already in them, albeit in a hidden form.

To most Christians, for most of the past two thousand years, it was unthinkable that you would choose to utterly destroy bodies destined for glory and already touched by grace. As they saw it, why would you burn hair or crush bones when God used the hair and bones of saints to heal

---

[17] Jerome, Letter 109.2.

cancer, cure infertility, or restore sight? If God saw fit to honor the remains of his holy ones in such a way, then surely he expects us to honor the remains of all his children, to treat them tenderly and with care and reverence.

Burial, Christians insisted, was peaceful. It was laying the body to rest until it could be reunited with its soul. Cremation, on the other hand, was violent; it was swiftly, forcefully, and utterly destroying a body in which the Body of Christ had dwelt.

As such, through nineteen long centuries, as bodies moved in and out of churches and were put to rest in underground catacombs, tombs, and churchyards, one thing remained constant: burial. Centuries passed, customs changed, funeral rites developed, and empires rose and fell, but no matter what, Christians buried their dead. Occasionally, they burned a heretic or witch and refused to bury the unfaithful or those who committed suicide in consecrated ground, but the bodies of everyone else were laid to rest whole.

Then, at the beginning of the twentieth century, that began to change. Why?

CHAPTER 11

CHANGING DIRECTIONS

In 785, the (soon-to-be) first Holy Roman Emperor, Charlemagne, was determined to bring the pagan Saxons into the Christian fold. He also was determined to keep them under his royal thumb and construct a new Christian empire in Western Europe. In an effort to accomplish both goals, he began enforcing a code of law that banned various pagan practices, including cremation. The law, which was the first of its kind, made cremation a capital offense: "If anyone follows pagan rites and causes the body of a dead man to be consumed by fire, and reduces his bones to ashes," it stated, "let him pay with his life."[1]

But that law didn't last any longer than the Carolingian Empire. After the empire crumbled near the end of the ninth century, no other European country or power explicitly banned or permitted cremation. They didn't need to. Nobody wanted to be cremated. And with no one so much

---

[1]   Henry R. Loyn and John Percival, *The Reign of Charlemagne* (New York: St. Martins, 1975), 52.

as talking about cremation, there was no need for a law that addressed it. It was simply a nonissue.

It stayed a nonissue for one thousand years. Then, in the nineteenth century, that began to change. Suddenly, lots of people were talking about it: French radicals and Italian Freemasons, German Socialists and Russian Bolsheviks, English doctors and American civil engineers.

A century later, people weren't just talking about it; they were doing it. The change came first in the UK and Europe. In 1905, 99.9 percent of the UK's population was buried.[2] By the late 1960s, that number had dropped to less than half. Today, it's less than a quarter, with 77 percent of people in the UK opting for cremation in 2017.[3]

The United States was slower to catch on. As late as 1960, fewer than 4 percent of Americans were cremated.[4] By 2018, though, that number had climbed to 53 percent. Forecasts have it climbing to 80 percent by 2035.[5]

What on earth happened? How did something that was unthinkable for the better part of the last two thousand years become the norm in so short a time?

The answer is complicated. Modernism, science, and sanitation concerns all played a part. So too did economics and culture. But, in the beginning, it wasn't any of those

---

[2] Thomas Laqueur, "The Burning Question: How Cremation Became Our Last Great Act of Self-Determination," *The Guardian*, October 30, 2015.

[3] "Cremation Statistics," Urns for Ashes, accessed December 21, 2019, www.urnsforashes.co.uk/cremation-statistics.

[4] Laqueur, "The Burning Question."

[5] "What is the 2018 Cremation Rate in the US?," US Funerals Online, accessed December 21, 2019, www.us-funerals.com/funeral-articles/2018-US-Cremation-Rate.html#.XWfgg5NKg_U.

things that started people talking about cremation. It was a hatred for the Church and what she taught about death and resurrection.

Revolutionary Fires

In faith, as in life, it's not uncommon for our enemies to understand us better than we understand ourselves. This was in large part true of the earliest supporters of cremation: the French revolutionaries, Freemasons, socialists, materialists, and atheists. They adamantly opposed the Catholic Church and what it taught. They thought Christian beliefs in the resurrection of the body and salvation in Jesus Christ were the height of foolishness and superstition. But they also knew they could oppose those teachings more effectively by simply opposing the reverent treatment of the body.

Changing the burial practices of the Christian people, they decided, would bear more fruit than simply engaging in sophisticated argumentation against Christian doctrines. They understood that more is caught than is taught, that culture influences the way people think and what we believe far more than homilies from pulpits do. And so, from the end of the eighteenth century on, you see the Church's enemies attempting to resurrect a practice that hadn't existed in the Christian world for a thousand years, all in the hopes of undermining the Christian faith.

This "resurrection" began during the French Revolution's infamous "Reign of Terror." In 1793, a group of royalists in the city of Toulon rose up and took back their city from the rulers of the Republic. The Republicans who didn't escape were imprisoned, including the thirty-nine-year-old French doctor and National Assemblyman, Charles Nicolas Beauvais de Préau.

Later that year, when Toulon fell to Napoleon and the armies of the Convention, de Préau was rescued, but liberation had come too late. In prison, de Préau had fallen ill. He never recovered, passing away four months later in Montpellier. The next day, Montpellier's Republican city officials announced that as a "martyr of liberty," de Préau would be publicly cremated. They then carried de Préau through the streets, with all pomp and circumstance, to the large wooden pyre they'd constructed in the middle of the city. The flames burned all day and into the night. In the morning, de Préau's ashes were taken to the Temple of Reason, a former Catholic Church that had been taken over by the "Cult of Reason" to use for explicitly anti-Catholic and pro-atheist activities.

De Préau's cremation was nothing less than a deliberate act of defiance on the part of the Republicans. It was a public assertion of their disregard for the Church and all of its "superstitions" about death.

A year later, the atheist Republicans asserted themselves again, explicitly making cremation legal and noting in the decree that "whereas the greater part of the people in antiquity burnt their dead," and since "this practice was abolished, or in any case fell into disuse, only because of religious influences," the burning of the dead would once more be a legitimate option for a people who had shaken off the shackles of religious superstition.[6]

---

[6] Laqueur, *The Work of the Dead*, 526.

As the secular historian Thomas Laqueur notes in his comprehensive history of human death and burial, *The Work of the Dead*:

> At issue in all this was not a particular view of the consequences of cremation versus burial: cleanliness, which would loom so large in later debates and in contemporary arguments for closing churchyards, played almost no role; there was no interest in technology. Cremation was meant to strike a blow at a millennium-old community of the dead buried in sacred ground and to offer a historically based alternative.[7]

Masons and More

Once the French revolutionaries decided that cremation was an effective form of protest against the Church, others followed suit.

In the 1860s and 1870s, it was the Italian Freemasons who led the push for cremation in their country. And yes, some Catholics like to blame everything on Freemason conspiracies. But even secular historians agree that the Masons were in on this one. Laqueur explains:

> The Masonic lodges of Italy, especially those of Milan and Turin, provided the institutional framework for advocacy of cremation, as well as for the

---

[7] Laqueur, *The Work of the Dead*, 527.

invention of new rituals and for construction of purpose-built crematoria. Jacob Salvatore Morelli, one of the main early publicists for cremation, was a freethinker, feminist, campaigner for more liberal divorce laws, and a Mason. The minister of the interior who gave permission for the first legal cremation in Italy, on 22 January 1876, was a Freemason, and so was Alberto Keller, the German Lutheran businessman who was cremated.[8]

Not coincidentally, Ludovico Brunetti, the inventor of the first modern crematory, who presented his techniques at the Vienna World Exposition in 1873, was also a Freemason.

It wasn't just the Freemasons, though, who supported cremation. Socialists in Germany and Bolsheviks in Russia also embraced it in equal measure. And they too weren't what you'd call fans of the Church. Laqueur writes:

> In 1920, when one might think more consequential matters were at hand, a small debate took place between German communists and social democrats about whether members of cremation societies should be obliged to remove their children from religious instruction in public schools. Yes, argued the communists, because at stake was cultural revolution; half steps were not enough.[9]

In Great Britain, it was actually a neo-Druidic priest

---

[8] Laqueur, *The Work of the Dead,* 528.
[9] Laqueur, *The Work of the Dead,* 530.

who succeeded in getting the British courts to affirm people's right to cremation. The Welshman William Price twice attempted (and once succeeded) in burning the body of his dead infant son. He was arrested both times, but the courts ruled that he had committed no crime: cremation had never been explicitly illegal. After Price's second arrest, though, it became explicitly legal. The following year, the first crematorium in Great Britain was built. More would follow.

Champions of Progress

It wasn't purely anti-religious sentiment that motivated the German and Russian advocates of cremation. In both places, an admiration for progress and technology went hand in hand with disdain for the Church. "Side by side with the car, tractor, and electrification—make way for cremation," proclaimed one Bolshevik publicity poster.[10]

In England and the United States, alongside atheists and materialists who shared the Socialists' and Bolsheviks' disdain for religious traditions, medical doctors and hygiene experts campaigned for cremation on public sanitation grounds. Some worried about corpses polluting water supplies. Others worried about corpses releasing poisonous gases into the air and harming the health of the community.

As they saw it, the dead were "refuse," garbage, biomedical waste that "constituted an acute problem for the military sanitary engineer in times of war and a chronic ev-

---

[10] Laqueur, *The Work of the Dead,* 530.

eryday problem for his counterpart in civil society."[11] With populations rising, they contended, states needed to devise a more efficient way than burial of disposing of this waste. Brunetti's crematorium in 1873 was the first successful step in that direction.

Sir Henry Thompson, one of Queen Victoria's physicians, witnessed Brunetti's work at the Vienna Exposition. He returned home and immediately established the British Cremation Society. Made up of scientists, medical doctors, and other illustrious public figures, such as the author Anthony Trollope, the society sponsored experiments to improve upon Brunetti's device. They also campaigned for widespread cremation, arguing that they wanted to "protect the living from corruption."[12]

In the twentieth century, ecological arguments added to cremation's popularity. Proponents contended that the earth simply didn't have enough room to bury its dead anymore. Cremation, they claimed, had become a necessity in a world with a population that continued to increase exponentially and where cities were becoming more overcrowded by the day.

The mounting cost of funerals didn't help either. As burying the dead became more and more expensive, cremation became both the economic and practical choice for families that didn't want to spend $5,000–$10,000 on a funeral (the average cost in 2016) and thousands more on a burial plot and headstone. Today, cremation costs between $800–$3,000, which, when finances are the only consider-

---

[11] Laqueur, *The Work of the Dead,* 513.
[12] Laqueur, *The Work of the Dead,* 513.

ation, is a significant difference.[13]

By the twenty-first century, globalization was added to the mix. Although some religious faiths—particularly Islam, but also Orthodox Judaism—prohibit cremation, others—including Hinduism and Buddhism—have always burned their dead. The more people of different cultures and faiths have intermingled, the more normal cremation has become in the West.

Champions of Man

Ultimately, it wasn't the Freemasons or science or globalization that tipped the scales in cremation's favor. It was modernism and postmodernism, two closely related ways of seeing the world, the human person, and the human body that came to dominate the West in the nineteenth and twentieth centuries.

During the many long centuries when Christians buried their dead, most saw the world through a sacramental lens. They recognized that everything in creation was made by God, loved by God, and had something to tell us about God. They knew that what God made, in part, revealed who God is.

They also knew this was and is true of the human person. Not only are men and women made in God's image, but Jesus Christ, the Son of God, became man. He took on a

---

[13] Norman L. Geisler and Douglas E. Potter, *What in Cremation Is Going On? A Christian Guide to Post Mortem Decisions* (Matthews, NC: Bastion Books, 2016), 48.

human body and a human nature. Then, after his death and Resurrection, he gave us his divine nature in the Eucharist. That makes the body of the baptized believer not only the image of God, but the temple of God.

Still, the faithful of old understood that while man might be the temple of God, he isn't God. God is God, Creator and Ruler, "the still point of the turning world," as T. S. Eliot once wrote.[14] God is at the center, his will is sovereign, and if man wants to become all that God made him to be, the only way to do that is by following God, by conforming our human wills to God's divine will, and letting God's grace animate our bodies and souls.

The modernists, however, upended that equation, putting man, not God, at the center of the universe and urging man to use his reason to exert greater control over the world. Which is why, in many ways, modernism was about power—man's power over nature, man's power over his fellow man, and even man's power over himself. The goal of modernism was to use that power to bring about greater health, wealth, and comfort for man.

But, as Pope Benedict XVI so clearly put it, "Man, in assigning to himself an inflated importance, damages his true self."[15]

Or, as Benedict's predecessor, Pope St. John Paul II, wrote:

[14] T. S. Eliot, "Burnt Norton."
[15] Benedict XVI, *Benedictus: Day by Day with Pope Benedict XVI*, ed. Peter John Cameron, O.P. (San Francisco: Ignatius Press, 2018), 254.

Once all reference to God has been removed, it is not surprising that the meaning of everything else becomes profoundly distorted. Nature itself, from being "mater" (mother), is now reduced to being "matter," and is subject to every kind of manipulation.[16]

When the modernists kicked God off center stage, the material world, which had once been imbued with divine meaning, became—in the eyes of the world—just another thing to control. Matter was no longer a witness to its Creator; it was just matter, something for man to use and manipulate.

Likewise, the body was no longer the image of God, the temple of the Holy Spirit, destined for resurrection on the last day. It too was just matter, valuable in life when it was useful—when it was young and strong, healthy and beautiful. But when it aged, when it became sick or weak, the body became a burden, no longer useful and no longer important.

The more this attitude trickled down from scholars and scientists into mainstream Western thought, the more thinkable the once unthinkable practice of cremation became. Of course you could burn that kind of body. What value was there in preserving it? What did the body really matter, once it had outlived its usefulness? It was just matter—and decaying matter at that.

Champions of the Self

Postmodernism followed modernism, but contrary to what

---

[16] John Paul II, *Evangelium Vitae* (1995), §22.

the name suggests, it didn't really reject modernism. Rather, postmodernism was a resounding affirmation of modernism's claim that man was at the center of everything. The only real difference was that postmodernism put the particular man, not man in general, at the center of the universe, arguing that the individual's feelings, beliefs, and experiences trumped everything else, even reason.

Rejecting universals for particulars, postmodernism's claim that nothing has meaning—that there is no truth, no goodness, no universally binding morality—just added fuel to the fire. After all, once God is out of the picture entirely and "my feelings," "my desires," "my will" become the only arbiters of what is true or right, why wouldn't I want my body burned and my ashes scattered over whatever garden or lake or city street had the most meaning to me in life? Resting in sacred ground, which has meaning to the community, to family, to people of faith, has far less attraction than resting along my favorite hiking path, which has meaning to me.

Modernism and postmodernism directly and powerfully contributed towards cremation's growing popularity. They made indirect contributions as well.

As marriage became about individual self-fulfillment and changeable feelings, divorce rates climbed and families split. As material success trumped community, moving far (and frequently) for work became more common. And as children came to be seen as burdens or commodities, not blessings, family sizes shrank. All these cultural trends, fed by modernism and postmodernism, meant that gravesites, where generations of your family members could visit you and remember you, held less appeal.

Likewise, modernism and postmodernism's focus on happiness in this life not only distracted people from thinking about the next life; it brought back the old fear of death that haunted the world before Jesus came. Death once more became a fearful end, not a glorious beginning. It signified the ultimate defeat, the end of all man's attempts to control his life and prosper.

As such, people more and more wanted to keep reminders of death far from them. Dead and dying bodies, bodies that once passed away in homes and were waked in family living rooms, were carted off to hospitals, nursing homes, and funeral parlors. Death, which had once been so familiar, became unfamiliar as increasing numbers of people sought to remove all evidence of it, including (and especially) the body. Cremation was the quickest, surest, and most direct route to that.

Reflecting on this tendency of modern and postmodern culture, Patricia Snow writes:

> The terrifying, implacable truth of man's condition—that his only hope is in God—is revealed in death. For people accustomed to editing their appearances and managing their public relations, the revelation is unbearable, and the idea of their stricken, mortified body on public view at a wake or funeral is insupportable. Cremation, in this view, asserts a kind of negative control precisely where control has been lost. If death reveals man's defeat, cremation destroys the evidence. It eliminates the alarming dead weight of the body; it bypasses the tedious, unsettling process of decay. What is left is

a small, portable box or jar: a symbol, or Ur-body, rather than the body itself.[17]

And what does the Catholic Church have to say to all this?

---

[17] Patricia Snow, "The Body and Christian Burial," *Communio* 39.3 (Fall 2012): 12.

CHAPTER 12

GRUDGING PERMISSION

As a theologian and university professor, it's easy for me to talk about ideas in the abstract. I love talking about ideas—about politics, theology, culture, and what different thinkers have to say. When I get going on a certain topic, it can be hard to shut me up. My students can attest to this!

But ideas rarely remain abstract. When they touch on our lives, our decisions, or the lives and decisions of people we love, they become personal. And it can be difficult to separate our personal experiences from the conversation. This is true for me, and I'm going to guess it's true for you.

Because of this very human habit of personalizing discussions, part of me was reluctant to write this book. Cremation hasn't just become more widespread in our culture at large; it's become more widespread in our Church as well. Which means, chances are, someone you know and love has chosen cremation at the end of his or her life. Maybe it's you who's chosen cremation and already talked to your loved ones about that decision or written it into your will. It's possible, before you made that decision, you talked to your priest or a deacon, and he told you it was fine, that the Church no longer had a problem with cremation, and Catholics have the green light to dispose of our bodies in whatever way we choose.

It's not that simple, though. Which is why we now need to look more closely at what the Church actually teaches about cremation and how she has responded to the culture's changing attitude toward the practice.

Conditions and Context

Before we can talk about how the Church's teaching on cremation has developed over the past century, we need to understand two important things about Church teaching.

First, broadly speaking, there are two types of Church teaching. There is Church doctrine, and there is Church discipline.

Doctrine refers to the teachings of the Church which have been revealed by God, belong to the Deposit of Faith, and are taught by the Magisterium. So, the nature of the Holy Trinity is a doctrine. The fact of the Incarnation is a doctrine. The Paschal Mystery, the sacraments, the Communion of Saints, the nature of the human person, all these are doctrines. And they are unchanging.

The Church has no authority to say that God isn't a Holy Trinity, that Jesus wasn't the Son of God, or that the Sacrament of Marriage can be anything other than the lifelong union of one man and one woman. It can't because these are all truths revealed by God in Scripture and Tradition. The Church simply can't change dogma. It might as well try to change the law of gravity.

Discipline is a different matter, though. Before his Ascension into heaven, Jesus entrusted his Apostles with the authority to govern his Church. Part of that governance is making rules that help the Church function effectively and help men and women live the faith and grow in holiness. The Church's canon law, her liturgical norms, requirement for priestly celibacy, and rules on fasting are all examples of Church disciplines. Unlike Church doctrine, they can and do change. The Church can adjust her disciplines to accommodate the changing needs, understandings, and challenges of different times and cultures. The goal remains the same: holiness. But how the Church helps her children reach that goal can differ in different ages.

Case in point? Friday abstinence. For hundreds of years, the Church required all Catholics everywhere to abstain from meat on Fridays. This small sacrifice, offered up on the day of the week where we remember Jesus's death, was a way for Catholics to unite themselves to Christ in his Passion. It was a small act of penance which drew us closer to him.

Then, in 1966, Pope St. Paul VI issued the apostolic constitution on fast and abstinence, *Paenitemini*. While he reiterated that "by divine law all the faithful are required to do penance," and that "abstinence is to be observed on every Friday which does not fall on a day of obligation," he also allowed national bishops conferences to "substitute abstinence and fast wholly or in part with other forms of penitence and especially works of charity and the exercises of piety."[1]

---

[1] Paul VI, *Paeniteminini*, Ch. 3 (1966).

In other words, the bishops of individual countries could decide that Catholics in their nation didn't have to abstain from meat on Fridays. They could abstain from chocolate or wine or they could pray a Rosary instead of fasting at all. The bishops could also allow individuals to decide for themselves how they would unite themselves to the suffering Christ on Fridays outside of Lent. And that is what most bishops' conferences did.

The reason *Paenitemini* gave for the change was that while abstaining from meat was a penitential act in wealthy nations, it was a way of life in poorer countries. By allowing bishops to adapt the required penance to best suit their flocks' needs, Paul VI recognized changing realities of the Catholic world.

When the change occurred, though, many people misunderstood it. As they saw it, eating meat on Fridays had been a sin before 1966, then wasn't a sin afterwards. But they misunderstood the sin. The sin never was eating meat. The sin was disobeying the Church's discipline. Once the Church changed the discipline, Catholics were still called to obey, just in a different way.

So, doctrines can't change. Disciplines can. That's the first thing we need to understand about Church teaching. The second is this: Church teaching does not unfold in a vacuum. There is nothing random about how and when the Magisterium defines a certain teaching or issues a certain rule. It is always done as a response to a particular problem, need, confusion, or circumstance.

This was the case in 325 at the Council of Nicaea, when the Church's bishops dogmatically declared that Jesus Christ was God's only begotten Son, consubstantial (of the same substance) with the Father. They did that not because it seemed like a fun thing to do at the time but because the heretic Arius had convinced many Christians, including bishops, that Jesus was not coeternal with the Father but rather had been created by him at some point in time.

This was also the case in 431 at the Council of Ephesus, when the bishops taught that Mary could rightfully be called "Mother of God" because Jesus was one divine Person, with a human nature and a divine nature. Again, the declaration was in response to a problem: the heretic Nestorius teaching that Jesus was somehow two persons, a Divine Person and a human person.

This continued to be the case throughout history, with the Church defining doctrines and promulgating rules in response to heresies, challenges, and changing circumstances within the life of the Church, from Paul VI writing *Humanae Vitae* in response to the development of the hormonal birth control pill to John Paul II developing the theology of the body in response to the sexual revolution and the culture's acceptance of contraception.

This also has been the case with the Church's teachings on burial and cremation.

Starting Position

In the early Church, when cremation was still the norm in the Roman Empire and the pagan Romans burned Christians, seeking to kill their hope in the resurrection, the Church Fathers and bishops made it clear that: 1) Cremation was not an obstacle to resurrection; God could resurrect our bodies even if our ashes were scattered to the four corners of the earth; and 2) Burial was a more fitting way for Christians to deal with their dead. In his *Octavius*, Minucius Felix summed up both points, declaring, "We do not fear loss from cremation even though we adopt the ancient and better custom of burial."[2]

Note: The Church Fathers said those things because Romans were burning Christians and because there were enough people who still burned their dead that the bishops had to teach converts the Christian way of doing things. That is to say, the early Christian teaching on the subject was in response to particular challenges and circumstances.

After those first several centuries, however, the Church's bishops stopped writing about cremation and burial because the need for them to do so went away. Nobody was cremating Christians or the Christian dead. Everyone was burying them. So, the need to reaffirm set disciplines about the practice didn't exist.

The issue popped up again, albeit briefly, in the fourteenth century, when some questioned how the government should deal with heretics. In 1300, Pope Boniface reaffirmed that cremation was no way to deal with faithful Christians. For witches and heretics, though, burning at the stake was permissible.[3]

Then, the issue didn't come up again until the end of the nineteenth century, when the Italian Freemasons and German socialists effectively forced the Church's hand on the issue.

---

[2] Minucius Felix, *Octavius* 34.
[3] See Geisler and Potter, 13.

In 1886, the Catholic Code of Canon Law was changed. The new law read:

> The bodies of the faithful must be buried, their cremation is forbidden. . . . Anyone who has requested that his body shall be cremated shall be deprived of ecclesiastical burial unless he has shown signs of repentance before death.[4]

That law was a direct response to those who promoted cremation with the desire of undermining the Church. The Church didn't think cremation a proper way to deal with the dead, but the even bigger problem in the Church's eyes was the anti-Catholic, anti-Christian agenda of cremation's supporters. The Church also outlawed membership in cremation societies for the same reason: "not as acts contrary to dogma, but as acts hostile to the Church."[5] As the 1908 *Catholic Encyclopedia* summed up the issue, cremation was, in effect, a "public profession of irreligion and materialism."[6]

Changing Course

The 1886 ban on cremation remained in effect for seventy-seven years. But in 1963 Pope Paul VI lifted that ban in *Piam et Constantem*. There, he reiterated the Church's ancient preference for burial and equally ancient antipathy for

---

[4] *Corpus Juris Canonici* 1203§1; 1240§1
[5] Laqueur, *The Work of the Dead,* 530.
[6] *Catholic Encyclopedia*, s.v. "Cremation."

cremation, explaining:

> The reverent, unbroken practice of burying the bodies of the faithful departed is something the Church has always taken pains to encourage. It has surrounded the practice with rites suited to bring out more clearly the symbolic and religious significance of burial and has threatened with penalties those who might attack the sound practice. The Church has especially employed such sanctions in the face of hate-inspired assaults against Christian practices and traditions by those who, imbued with the animosity of their secret societies, sought to replace burial by cremation. This practice was meant to be a symbol of their antagonistic denial of Christian dogma, above all of the resurrection of the dead and the immortality of the soul.[7]

Paul VI then goes on to note that those "hate-inspired assaults" which use the dead as a weapon against the Church had died down and the number of faithful Christians imploring the Church to allow cremation had increased "for reasons of health, economics, or other reasons involving private or public order."[8] *Piam et Constantem* is a sort of compromise response to those requests.

On the one hand, it insists that burial remain the norm:

All necessary measures must be taken to preserve

---

[7] Holy Office, *Piam et Constantem* (1963), §3366.

[8] Holy Office, *Piam et Constantem*, §3366.

the practice of reverently burying the faithful departed. Accordingly, through proper instruction and persuasion Ordinaries are to ensure that the faithful refrain from cremation and not discontinue the practice of burial except when forced to do so by necessity.[9]

But, at the same time, as long as persons are not seeking cremation because of "a denial of Christian dogmas, the animosity of a secret society, or hatred of the Catholic religion and the Church," and are choosing it instead only "when forced to do so by necessity," then cremation is permitted.[10]

Before closing, the pope adds one more reminder about the importance of burial: "The devout attitude of the faithful toward the ecclesiastical tradition must be kept from being harmed and the Church's adverse attitude toward cremation must be clearly evident."[11]

Under exactly what conditions the pope thought people would choose cremation isn't entirely clear. Perhaps in atheist or communist countries, where cremation was forced upon the faithful by the state? Maybe when transporting a body for burial put an undue burden on a family? Either way, he didn't seem to expect the majority of the faithful to start opting for cremation. But because he didn't spell out exactly what circumstances made cremation permissible, he effectively made all circumstances permissible.

Patricia Snow writes:

---

[9] Holy Office, *Piam et Constantem*, §3367.
[10] Holy Office, *Piam et Constantem*, §3368.
[11] Holy Office, *Piam et Constantem*, §3370.

But ultimately, no burden is placed on the petitioner at all. His circumstances do not need to be exceptional; they need only to be ordinary. So long as he is not an inflammatory atheist, a militant Mason, or a dissenter from Church teaching—and the working assumption is that he is none of these—he can cremate.[12]

Twenty years later, the 1983 revised Code of Canon Law got no more specific. Instead, it simply summarized *Piam et Constantem's* conclusions: "The Church earnestly recommends that the pious custom of burial be retained; it does not however forbid cremation, unless it is chosen for reasons which are contrary to Christian teaching."[13]

Over the next two decades, more documents would be released from the Church on the topic, including the 1989 English edition of the *Order of Christian Funerals*; *Reflections on the Body, Cremation, and Catholic Funeral Rites*, issued in 1997 by the United States Conference of Catholic Bishops; and in 1993, the *Catechism of the Catholic Church*. Across the board, Snow tells us:

Each of these documents urges, strongly prefers, and earnestly recommends that Catholics continue the reverent and unbroken (piam et constantem) practice of burying the bodies of the faithful dead. The documents allow for cremation, but in language that is guarded and implicitly censorious:

---

[12] Snow, "The Body and Christian Burial," 400.
[13] Code of Canon Law, canon 1176§3.

the Church does not forbid cremation; she does not object to it where there is an upright motive, based on serious reasons; she makes allowance for it in cases of necessity; and so on. At every point in her gradual relaxation of the ban, the Church has taken the opportunity to reaffirm her traditional view, and has urged her priests and bishops to teach the same.[14]

Clarifying the Course

It seems that all those affirmations of burial fell on deaf ears. With each passing decade the number of Catholics seeking cremation rose, with at least a third of all Catholics opting for cremation by 2013.[15]

In 2016, the Vatican once more issued a document touching on cremation and once more noted that it "insistently recommends that the bodies of the deceased be buried in cemeteries or other sacred places." It went on to explain that "burial is above all the most fitting way to express faith and hope in the resurrection of the body" and that by "burying the bodies of the faithful, the Church confirms her faith in the resurrection of the body, and intends to show the great dignity of the human body as an integral part of the human

---

[14] Snow, "The Body and Christian Burial," 399.
[15] Catholic Advance, "Cremation Numbers Rising; Burial of a Body Still Preferred by the Church," Catholic Diocese of Wichita, September 25, 2019, https://catholicdioceseofwichita.org/cremation-numbers-rising-burial-of-a-body-still-preferred-by-the-church.

person whose body forms part of their identity."[16]

It also explains that "burial in a cemetery or another sacred place adequately corresponds to the piety and respect owed to the bodies of the faithful departed who through Baptism have become temples of the Holy Spirit," that "the Church considers the burial of the dead one of the corporal works of mercy," and that burial both encourages prayers for the dead and is a perpetual reminder of the communion of the saints:

> Through the practice of burying the dead in cemeteries, in churches or their environs, Christian tradition has upheld the relationship between the living and the dead and has opposed any tendency to minimize, or relegate to the purely private sphere, the event of death and the meaning it has for Christians.[17]

At the same time, the document acknowledged that the trend toward cremation has become almost "unstoppable" and, in recognition of that, laid out the terms for how cremated ashes are to be treated. Quite simply, they are to be kept together—not scattered across land, air, or sea, not divided among friends or family members, and not turned into pieces of jewelry or other memorabilia. Also, they are

---

[16] Congregation for the Doctrine of the Faith, "Instruction regarding the burial of the deceased and the conservation of the ashes in the case of cremation" (2016), §3.

[17] Congregation for the Doctrine of the Faith, "Instruction regarding the burial of the deceased and the conservation of the ashes in the case of cremation," §3.

to be laid to rest in a sacred place—a church, a cemetery, or a columbarium—not retained in a domestic residence. It explains:

> From the earliest times, Christians have desired that the faithful departed become the objects of the Christian community's prayers and remembrance. Their tombs have become places of prayer, remembrance and reflection. The faithful departed remain part of the Church who believes "in the communion of all the faithful of Christ, those who are pilgrims on earth, the dead who are being purified, and the blessed in heaven, all together forming one Church."[18]

And that's where the Church stands today. It does not approve of cremation; it permits it. It does not permit the scattering of ashes or their retention in homes; it forbids it. It considers burial the most fitting way to care for the bodies of the dead until they rise again on the last day and urges us to follow that recommendation.

Whether or not we listen to the Church matters. Not to our bodies. God can take care of whatever we do to those. But it matters for us. It matters for the Church. And it matters for our culture.

Although the Church has repeatedly said that she doesn't recommend cremation, that it isn't fitting, that burial is the

---

[18] Congregation for the Doctrine of the Faith, "Instruction regarding the burial of the deceased and the conservation of the ashes in the case of cremation," §5.

preferred way for Christians to care for their bodies after death, the Church still has permitted it. And that permitting, combined with the widespread embrace of the practice, has become its own kind of teaching. In this world, actions speak louder than words. More is caught than is taught. And that has led to widespread confusion—not just about what the Church teaches on burial and cremation, but much more fundamentally, what the Church teaches about the resurrection and the body itself.

Cremation teaches people lessons about the body that are directly contrary to what the Church actually believes. It teaches that the body is disposable. It teaches that the body is not an integral part of the human person. And it teaches that the body has no value once the soul is gone—that body has run its course, and there will be nothing more for it. No resurrection. No transformation. No glorification.

Cremation communicates one truth about the body. Burial communicates another. And which truth we believe has implications not just for our death, but for our life.

CHAPTER 13

THE LOGIC OF LOVE

One of the words I've circled back to in chapter after chapter as I've written this book is "fittingness." It's a word you see often in the writings of the Church Fathers as they grappled with the mysteries of the faith. They were trying to make sense of ideas that, at the time, were entirely new and entirely shocking: God becoming man; God dying on a cross; God giving himself to us through bread that had become Body.

Two thousand years later, we tend to take these mysteries for granted. Of course, God became man. Of course, God died on a cross to atone for our sins. Of course, bread becomes body in the Eucharist. But there really is no "of course" about any of it. God didn't have to do any of those things. There was nothing necessary about the Incarnation. There was nothing necessary about the Paschal Mystery. There was nothing necessary about the Eucharist. There was actually nothing necessary about creation—about God creating the world in seven days or seventy million days.

Theology isn't geometry or physics. The rules are different. And when you start grappling with the mysteries that come to us through Divine Revelation, you realize there is nothing strictly necessary about anything in theology. Everything God has done in salvation history—from creating the world and becoming man to establishing a Church and instituting the sacraments—has been done freely, out of his goodness and love. God didn't have to do any of it. None of it was necessary. So why did he do it? How do we make sense of one incredible truth after another—from creation to the resurrection of our own bodies?

That's what the early Church Fathers had to discover.

A Different Kind of Catechesis

Over the last thousand years, theologians have had it pretty easy. We've haven't had to figure out, whole cloth, how to make the incomprehensible comprehensible. The Church Fathers already did that for us. We stand on the shoulders of giants. They stood on entirely new ground. They had to grapple with truths that humanity had never even imagined, and they also had to come up with ways to help people understand those truths.

What they came up with very often were arguments from fittingness. Since none of God's actions in time were necessary, they reasoned, then they at least had to be fitting. The word they used was *conveniens*, which looks like the English word convenience but is more about what is appropriate, consistent, or harmonious. The idea is that what God does in the economy of salvation reflects who God is. Simply put, God is consistent. He acts in accord with his nature. There is an internal logic to all of his actions in time that flows from who God is in all eternity. And because God is love, that logic is the logic of love.

The Church Fathers used this way of doing theology to help people understand the deepest truths about God—about who he is and why he did what he did in salvation history. They showed how the logic of love illuminated mysteries like the Trinity and the Incarnation. What they didn't do, though, was apply it to morality. There was no real need to do that. The Ten Commandments and the moral law laid out in biblical passages like the Sermon on the Mount seemed straightforward enough. Most Christians didn't need to be convinced that abortion or homosexuality or stealing or lying was wrong.

That's not the case today, though. Modernism and post-modernism have decimated our collective belief in both the natural law and moral law. They've also decimated the culture that arose long ago from a people who believed in Christ's Resurrection and our own. And so, what a number of Catholic writers and theologians have proposed is that we take a page from the Church Fathers' playbook and start using arguments from fittingness once again. Only this time, we use them not to help us understand just who God is and why he's done what he's done, but also how to understand who we are and how we are to live in this world.

This type of catechesis is what I've tried to do in this book. We've looked at what life is and what death is, what the body is and for what purpose God made it. We've also looked at what Scripture and Church history tell us about death, resurrection, and the dignity of the body. And from all that, we've seen why the Church teaches what she does about both cremation and burial—that the one doesn't make resurrection impossible, so it can be permitted, but that the other more fully reflects the truth of the body and the fate that awaits it, so it is what's recommended.

This doesn't just apply to burial though. We can apply this method of catechesis to every aspect of human existence: to family life and sexual morality, eating and drinking, business and economics, politics and liturgy, music and sports. We can look at the whole of life in light of God's love and discern the most fitting responses to that love in every area of life.

Not only can we do this, we should do this. God doesn't want our faith to be something isolated from the rest of our day. He wants our faith to transform every aspect of our lives—everything we do in our bodies, everything we do in this world. And that same logic of love that helps us make sense of who God is and what he's done in salvation history can help us make sense of everything the Church teaches about morality and the virtues. In a world that has lost its bearings and no longer finds arguments from authority persuasive, arguments from fittingness, arguments rooted in the logic of love, can be far more effective.

God's love has reached down so far and stretched itself beyond anything we can imagine. The more we meditate on that love, the more we strive to imitate that love, the more we live in that love, the more others can see how that love encompasses them as well. This book focuses on just one small teaching that makes sense in light of God's love. But you could fill a library with what's left to say on the subject.

A Holy Bridge

Back to the subject at hand, though: the body.

We've seen, as I keep saying, that more is caught than is taught. More is known than is shown. And so, if we want people to understand these truths about the body, the human person, and our eternal destiny, if we want them to believe these truths and live them, we have a responsibility to teach them through our example. We need to do exactly what those French revolutionaries and Freemasons aimed to do long ago, but with the exact opposite goal.

The Church's enemies thought that by burning bodies, they could undermine people's faith in the resurrection and the Catholic faith itself. And they were right. But, with grace, we can reverse course. By burying our bodies, by treating them with love, reverence, and gratitude, we can help restore people's faith in the resurrection, the dignity of the body, the dignity of the person, and God's Fatherly love.

Catholics often accuse the culture of being too materialistic. But our real problem is that the culture isn't materialistic enough. We undervalue matter. We undervalue how God works through the physical to affect the spiritual. Most of all, we undervalue the body.

We live in a world that primarily sees the body as one of two things: a burden or a barrier. People see the body as a burden because it grows sick, it grows old, it dies. It fails all of us by not being strong enough or fast enough or attractive enough; by not being fertile enough or by being too fertile; by limiting us in a thousand different ways and preventing us from living the life we think we should be living.

People also see the body as a barrier or a boundary. We

struggle to communicate to others who we really are and we struggle to understand who others really are. We long for communion, but don't know how to give ourselves in the right way or receive the gift of others. We think we've been hemmed in by the body and long for the day we can be free of it.

But the Church proposes to us another way of seeing the body—as a bridge.

Our body isn't the barrier that prevents others from knowing us. It's the bridge that *allows* others to know us. By our words and gestures, facial expressions and actions, our bodies communicate the invisible truths about who we are to the world. Our bodies make us known in time and space. They allow us to serve others and be served by them.

Our bodies also allow others to see something of God. Made in the image of God, every body of every person expresses a profound truth about who God is. In our bodies' ability to create and give and love, they reflect a God who is the Creator, the giver of all good gifts, and love himself. Moreover, in their ability to bring new life into the world, they image a God who is, from all eternity, life-giving love.

Everything about our bodies—their beauty, their strength, their tenderness, their endurance, their swiftness, their grace, their life-giving capacity—all of it reflects truths about who we are and who God is. They are the bridge by which the invisible passes into the visible and by which the eternal passes into the temporal. God reached us by entering time and taking on a body. Grace reaches our souls by traveling through our body. And grace reaches out into the world by traveling back through our bodies—through our hands, feet, eyes, and mouths. God's love, God's kindness,

God's mercy, and God's care are made manifest in the world through our love, our kindness, our mercy, and our care.

Every single day, our bodies have the capacity to convey some of the most important truths about God and man to the world. Even in death, they speak about who we are. They attest to our weakness and our need for Christ. But they also remind us that there is more to come. The body at rest in death is not meant to stay at rest. The very wrongness we feel when we look at the body of a person who was just alive helps us know that death isn't the end. More is still to come. And when we respond to that, when we treat the body for what it is and for what it was in life, burying it, not burning it, our bodies continue to teach the world about the dignity of the human person and the extraordinary fate that awaits us on the last day.

Homecoming

This past August, I was away from home, speaking at a conference. Around midnight, I got back to the hotel and called my wife Kimberly to check in on her. After I told her about my day, I asked about hers.

"Well, I'm in the ER," she began, "I was having some pain, so they're doing some tests."

To understand why she waited to drop that bomb on me, you'd have to know Kimberly. She is the strongest woman I know and takes things like that in stride. Me? Not so much. I immediately went into a panic, looking for flights that could get me home earlier. I was a wreck until I made it to the hospital the next day.

As it turns out, she had gallstones, and emergency surgery took care of them. It wasn't, in the grand scheme of things, all that serious, but it still gave me the scare of my life. I was going through draft chapters of this book at the time, and so death, unfortunately, was a little too much on my mind.

Even today, I can't shake the image of Kimberly in a hospital bed, and I can't stop thinking about how precious and beautiful every inch of her is. The thought of burning that body, of letting an ounce of harm come to it, even after her soul left it, strikes me as sheer madness. That is the body of my bride. That is the body that was home to all six of our children on earth, plus our three other miscarried loved ones. For that alone it is a sacred place, and to burn it would be unimaginable to me.

Beyond all the theological reasons for Mary's Assumption into heaven, there is a very human reason Jesus never let decay touch his mother's body. It had been his home for nine months. And you don't burn your home just because you no longer live in it.

When we receive the Eucharist, like Mary, each of us holds Jesus Christ, body and soul, within us. Physically, he doesn't stay long. Maybe twenty minutes at the outside. But as long as we remain in grace, his Spirit remains. And our bodies are never the same. The body in sanctifying grace is always a temple. But every body that has ever received Christ in the Eucharist is also his home.

Thinking about this has also got me thinking about my grandma, and all I didn't say, both when I preached that funeral homily long ago and when I knew her in life. I wish I could go back, give her just one more hug, and apologize.

I never appreciated what a gift she was, what a mystery she was, what a mystery we all are.

Each and every one of our bodies was made for a life. We were made for a destiny, for a glory, at which all the words in this book have only begun to hint. And we don't appreciate them enough. We don't appreciate them rightly. We worship the body when we should revere it. We try to control the body when we should care for it. We resent the body when we should praise God every minute of every day for it.

As the miracle-working bodies of the saints remind us, even in death grace lingers about our bodies. Like a Church after the tabernacle is removed, the body remains the place where heaven and earth, time and eternity, met. And it holds within it the potential for them to meet again.

Is it permissible to burn the body? Yes, it is. But when you understand what the body is, what it does, and what it's made for, when you truly see the body as it is now and as it will be, that makes burning it unthinkable.

Again, though, that's not just true about the body. When we use Scripture and Tradition and the light of faith to look more deeply at ourselves, our world, and the truths of Revelation, astonishment follows. We think we know the mysteries of the faith, but all the theologians writing in all the years since Jesus lived haven't scratched the surface of how truly glorious these mysteries are. There is so much more to see, so much more to comprehend, and in an age of scandal and heartbreak in the Church, asking Christ to help us see more deeply into the truths of the faith is the best antidote I know of to the temptation to give up on the faith.

If we stare into the darkness, our eyes will grow used to

the dark, and we will see more of what the darkness hides. But the same holds true for the light. If we stare into the light, our capacity for seeing everything touched by the light grows. And the more we see how the light of Christ illuminates all of life, the more we can live our lives in accord with that light, the more we can be transformed by that light, and the more we can reflect that light.

Jesus spent three years preaching and healing people in and around Judea. He spent thirty years, though, playing and working, eating and sleeping in Nazareth. During those thirty years, he wasn't waiting to start the work of redeeming the world. He was redeeming the world. He was redeeming the world in ways we can't even imagine, and he was doing it through the ordinary work of a carpenter, the ordinary routines of a family, the ordinary prayers of a first-century Jewish man.

That knowledge should stop us in our tracks. It should force us to reevaluate everything we do in these bodies of ours. It should force us to reexamine the power, beauty, and glory of the lives we live now. It also should remind us that the beauties and glories of this life, the beauties and glories of this body, don't hold a candle to the beauties and glories of what awaits us in the life to come. That is the life for which we hope. That is the life for which we were made. That is the life that is fully a life.

POSTSCRIPT

The Hour of Our Death

Easter 2020 was always the scheduled release date for this book. Emily and I worked on it during the summer of 2019, finished our edits over Christmas, and on February 28, 2020, a week before the book was scheduled to go to press, filmed an episode about it for the television show *Franciscan Presents*. Then, days later, the coronavirus known as COVID-19 started spreading across the United States. And I stopped the presses.

I've never done that with a book before. But I didn't want to put this book into the hands of people still reeling from both the rapid spread of the virus and the societal changes that have followed without adding a few final thoughts. Because death, for many of us, just became a whole lot less abstract and life far more uncertain.

In so many ways, the situation in which our world suddenly finds itself is unprecedented. But, in others ways, it feels very familiar.

I'm thinking, of course, of September 11, 2001. I still remember the shock and sorrow I felt watching the Twin Towers fall. I also remember the uncertainty of the days that followed. We didn't know then if and when the attacks would end. We didn't know what more the terrorists had in store for our country. All we knew was that in the space of a few hours, thousands of our fellow Americans died horrible deaths. And we were scared.

For many of us, 9/11 was a wake-up call—a reminder that our comfortable settled lives could be upended in a moment, that death can always be just one heartbeat away, and that nothing in this world is ever certain, least of all tomorrow.

Not long after the Towers fell, Kimberly and I gathered the children to pray. Like us, they were struggling to make sense of what had happened and Hannah, who had just turned 13, had a question for me.

"Dad," she said, "I have to know—are we all going to die?"

"Yes," I responded. "100 percent. Definitely."

All the kids, looked at me, startled. I paused. Then, I continued. "Everyone's going to die, Hannah. But I don't think it will be today."

I added, "But the important thing, the real question, is *not* are we going to die, but are we ready to die?"

Later, after we finished our prayers, I turned the conversation back to Hannah's question. I explained that while the mortality rate for each of us is 100 percent, the immortality rate for each of us is also 100 percent. Death is not the end. Not for anyone. Every person who has ever lived is still alive in one state or another—a state of grace or a state of disgrace.

I then referenced St. John Henry Newman's sermon on "The Individuality of the Soul." In it, he reminds us:

> All those millions upon millions of human beings who ever trod the earth and saw the sun successively, are at this very moment in existence all together. This, I think, you will grant we do not duly realize. All those Canaanites, whom the children of Israel slew, every one of them is somewhere in the universe, now at this moment, where God has assigned him a place.[1]

I'm not sure how much of an impression the Newman sermon made on the kids at the time, but it has stayed with me, this vision of the masses of humanity—from Adam and Eve and the men and women who died on 9/11 to those dying, even as I write, from a horrible virus that literally takes your breath away. As I watch the news unfold, I can't help but think of them all, still living, still waiting, still anticipating, whether in fear or hope, the Last Day.

From Curse to Blessing

In death, the divide between hope and fear is unbridgeable. Each of the waiting dead knows what will happen to them at the time of the Final Judgment. They know if their body will be resurrected to death or to life. Those who hope, hope

---

[1] John Henry Newman, "The Individuality of the Soul," *Parochial and Plain Sermons* (San Francisco: Ignatius Press, 1997), 786.

with certainty. Those who fear, fear with equal certainty. They all know what they freely chose in life—heaven or hell—and they know the time for making another choice has passed. Christ the Judge has pronounced their fate, and that fate is sealed.

But here and now, the chasm between hope and fear can be crossed. We don't have to dread the end of this earthly life. We don't have to live in terror about what comes after we close our eyes for the last time. No matter how far we've run from God, no matter how often we've chosen against him and his ways, we still have time to make another choice. Like the Prodigal Son, we can return to the Father's house and know that he will welcome us with open arms, transforming our fear of death into hope for life.

The fear so many of us feel in the face of death is, of course, natural. We weren't made for death. We were made for life.

But Jesus came to release us from our fear of death. The loving obedience he offered on the cross atoned for our sins and opened the gates to Heaven for all who follow him. But it also changed the very meaning of death for those united to him. It "transformed the curse of death into a blessing," making death the door that leads to everlasting life with God (CCC 1009).

Quoting Saint Paul, the Catechism explains:

> Because of Christ, Christian death has a positive meaning: "For to me to live is Christ, and to die is gain." . . . What is essentially new about Christian death is this: through Baptism, the Christian has already 'died with Christ' sacramentally, in order

to live a new life; and if we die in Christ's grace, physical death completes this "dying with Christ" and so completes our incorporation into him in his redeeming act. (1010)

That is to say, for those who die in Christ's grace, death isn't a solitary act; it's "a participation in the death of the Lord," and when we die with the Lord, we also rise with the Lord; we participate in his resurrection (CCC 1006).

This participation changes everything. The Church's liturgy reminds us of this. "Lord, for your faithful people life is changed, not ended," we hear the priest say at funeral Masses. "When the body of our earthly dwelling lies in death we gain an everlasting dwelling place in heaven."

When we know death is not the end, when we know that death is just the beginning of everlasting joy, everlasting life, and everlasting communion with the One we love, hope drives out fear. It makes us long for death. It makes us long to be with Christ in a world where there is no suffering, no pain, no loss. This is why St. Francis could pray:

Praised are you, my Lord, for our sister bodily Death,
from whom no living man can escape.
Woe on those who will die in mortal sin!
Blessed are they who will be found
in your most holy will,
for the second death will not harm them. (CCC 1014)

Knowing death is not the end also makes us long for something else. It makes us long to share our hope with others.

Preparing the Way

If my life follows its natural course, I will leave this world before my children and likely before Kimberly, too. I want to be with Christ. But I also want to be with them. I want us all to experience the joy of the Beatific Vision together. That desire—for all of us to be together in Heaven, fully alive, in body and soul—has shaped everything about my life: the kind of husband and father I am, the work I do, the prayers I offer—all of it.

I strive to love my wife in such a way that both she and I can more freely and joyfully say yes to all Christ asks of us. I try to love my children in such a way that they experience the love of the Father through me, and trust him all the more for that experience. I teach and write and speak with the hope that my students around the world will one day get to sit with me at the table of the Lamb. And I pray, daily, hourly, for the grace to be ready to go to Jesus when he calls me home. I also pray for the souls of my friends and loved ones, both those who are alive and those who are dead.

This is the opposite of how the world tells us to live. The world tells us to eat, drink, and make merry, for tomorrow we may die. The world sees death as the end, with only darkness to follow. The Church, however, tells us to love, sacrifice, serve, and pray, so that tomorrow we might live. It sees death not so much as an end, but as a beginning, and urges us to both remain in Christ's grace and ask him for the graces to do so. It also urges us to call upon the saints—those who have obtained the life for which we long—and ask for their prayers. The Catechism notes:

The Church encourages us to prepare ourselves for the hour of our death. In the ancient litany of the saints, for instance, she has us pray: "From a sudden and unforeseen death, deliver us, O Lord"; to ask the Mother of God to intercede for us "at the hour of our death" in the *Hail Mary*; and to entrust ourselves to St. Joseph, the patron of a happy death. (CCC 1014)

But it's not just about us, about our soul and our death. The Church encourages us to hope and pray for all those we've lost. She asks us not to presume that anyone has gone straight to heaven or hell, but rather to petition God with loving confidence on their behalf.

Our prayers and sacrifices for loved ones who've gone before us have real efficacy. They can bring comfort and consolation to those suffering from the purification that comes in purgatory, and they can bring about their final release from that purification, helping them experience at long last the loving gaze of the Father. The Catechism tells us:

This teaching is . . . based on the practice of prayer for the dead, already mentioned in Sacred Scripture: "Therefore [Judas Maccabeus] made atonement for the dead, that they might be delivered from their sin." From the beginning the Church has honored the memory of the dead and offered prayers in suffrage for them, above all the Eucharistic sacrifice, so that, thus purified, they may attain the beatific vision of God. The Church also commends almsgiving, indulgences, and works of penance undertaken on behalf of the dead. (CCC 1032)

These prayers also bring comfort to us, who are left behind. In his First Letter to the Thessalonians, Saint Paul reminded the Christian community that they were not to "grieve as others do who have no hope" (4:13). He didn't tell them not to grieve. Grief is a normal, natural human emotion. We want to be with the people we love, so of course we grieve them when they leave us. But, when we grieve, we grieve with hope. We grieve, hoping they clung to Christ to the last or chose him at the last. We grieve, hoping that our prayers for the faithful departed can assist them on their journey home to the Father's house. And we grieve, hoping that someday we will all be together again, sharing in the joy and peace and life that is promised to all in Heaven.

I can't overstate how important our prayers for the faithful departed are—for them and us. When grief takes hold of our hearts, when we long to be reunited with the ones we've lost, we have the comfort of knowing we can take direct action now to assist all those we've loved who are enduring their final purification in purgatory.

Whether they died in visible communion with the Church or not, whether they were buried according to the mind of the Church or not, we can still help them. We can offer up penances great and small for them, say Rosaries for them, and obtain indulgences for them. We also can visit cemeteries and pray for them. And we can offer the traditional prayer of the Church for the dead at every meal, whether before we eat or after: "And may the souls of the faithful departed, through the mercy of God, rest in peace."

Most of all, we can have Masses offered for those we've lost.

The Power of the Mass

No prayer is more powerful than the Mass, and there is no greater way to show our love for our dead than to have Masses said for them. This is the ancient teaching of the Church, and the ancient practice of the faithful. Writing in the sixth century, Pope St. Gregory the Great noted that:

> The holy Sacrifice of Christ, our saving Victim, brings great benefits to souls even after death, provided their sins can be pardoned in the life to come. For this reason the souls of the dead sometimes beg to have Masses offered for them.[2]

Gregory went on to recall the story of an old priest who was assisted daily at the baths by a mysterious stranger. One day, he attempted to thank the stranger with an offering of bread. But instead of accepting it, the stranger explained that in life he had been the owner of the baths and treated others cruelly. Now, his punishment was to serve those who came to the baths.

He then said to the old priest, "If you wish to do something for me, then offer this bread to almighty God, and so make intercession for me, a sinner. When you come back

---

[2] Gregory the Great, *Dialogues*, trans. John Zimmerman, OSB (Washington, DC: Catholic University of America Press, 1959), 266.

and do not find me here, you will know that your prayers have been heard."[3]

As soon as the stranger finished speaking, he disappeared from sight. The kindly old priest spent the next week praying for the man and offering Mass daily for him. When he returned to the bath a week later, there was no sign of the man. His punishment had been lifted and he had gone to God.

Gregory also told the story of a monk, Justus, who had died, estranged from his community. His brother monks came to Gregory and asked him what they could do to help Justus, so Gregory ordered that a Mass be said for the deceased monk every day for thirty days. At the end of those thirty days, Gregory writes, "Justus appeared to his brother Copiosus, who asked him at once why he came and how he was. 'Up to this moment I was in misery,' he said, 'but now I am well, because this morning I was admitted to communion.'"[4]

This practice of having thirty Masses offered for the dead continues to this day in numerous religious orders, and is referred to as "Gregorian Masses." Other Masses for the dead are offered in every parish in the world, although as the numbers of the faithful shrink, so too do the number of Masses being offered for departed loved ones.

Resurrecting this tradition in our families and communities is easily the most important and powerful thing we can do to help those we've lost. We cannot forget that how we honor and love our dead doesn't end with their burial.

---

[3] Gregory the Great, *Dialogues*, 267.
[4] Gregory the Great, *Dialogues*, 269.

It goes on, every day of our life, until, God willing, we see them again.

* * *

The first Christians—our fathers and mothers in the faith—didn't fear death; they anticipated it. Many of them ran toward it, wanting nothing more than to begin what C. S. Lewis described as "Chapter One of the Great Story, which no one on Earth has read: which goes on forever: in which every chapter is better than the one before."[5]

People often refer to the Gospel or even salvation history as "the greatest story ever told." But it's not really. It's just the introduction. Or a prelude. What comes after this life, when the blessed enter into the Beatific Vision and see in the Father's eyes the story of their life, of everyone's lives, of all the world, that will be the greatest story ever told, the one to which every other story belongs, the story that makes sense of all the stories, the story we've been waiting our whole lives to hear.

Right now, as Christians, we're called to imitate those first Christians. We may or may not be called to run toward death in the arena or the hospital ward. But we are most certainly called to set aside our fear of death and live in hope. We are called to hope that we will see our lost loved ones again and to hope that with them, one day, we will rest in the arms of our Father.

We're also called to hope in the God who took the single greatest evil ever perpetrated—the crucifixion of our Lord—and brought out of it the single greatest good the world has ever known: the redemption of humanity. If God

---

[5]   C. S. Lewis, *The Last Battle* (New York: Harper Collins, 1954), 211.

can bring goodness and glory and beauty and life out of that kind of evil, he most certainly can bring goodness and glory and beauty and life out of the evil we presently face.

Hope is what will sustain us in the days yet to come. It also will make it possible for us to experience joy in this day, no matter what sorrows presently afflict us.

Again, death is not the end. We were made for life. We were made for joy. And in Christ, that life and joy will be ours. In Christ, that life and joy are already ours. Death brings the fulfillment of that life and joy, but we can live in it now. Even in the midst of grief. Even in the midst of war. Even in the midst of plagues and poverty and confusion. If we are in Christ, we have nothing to fear from the terrors of the world. They cannot kill the life inside us. They cannot deprive us of the joy that is ours. They cannot rob us of the hope that fills us—the hope of eternal life.

> *"O death, where is thy sting?"*
> 1 Corinthians 15:55

Scott Hahn
March 19, 2020
Solemnity of St. Joseph, Patron of a Holy Death